PENGUIN BOOKS

1414

HOW CAN YOU BEAR TO BE HUMAN?

NICOLAS BENTLEY

How can you bear to

With an Introduction by Malcolm Muggeridge

be HUMAN? NICOLAS BENTLEY.

PENGUIN BOOKS

Penguin Books Ltd, Harmondsworth, Middlesex
AUSTRALIA: Penguin Books Pty Ltd, 762 Whitehorse Road,
Mitcham, Victoria

—

First published by André Deutsch 1957
Published by Penguin Books 1959
Reprinted 1961

—

Made and printed in Great Britain
by Richard Clay & Company, Ltd,
Bungay, Suffolk

To the lady on page 33, bless her!

ACKNOWLEDGEMENTS

TIME and taste wait for no man, and in order not to be left too far behind by either, I have made a few minor changes in some of the pieces in this book since their first appearance elsewhere. For their previous publication and for permission to include them here, I am indebted to André Deutsch Ltd, Michael Joseph Ltd, Victor Gollancz Ltd, George Routledge & Sons Ltd, Allan Wingate Ltd; and to the editors of the *Daily Graphic*, the *Egyptian Gazette*, *Ford Times*, *Future*, *Homes and Gardens*, *Lilliput*, the *New Statesman*, *News Chronicle*, *Punch*, the *Queen*, *Sunday Express*, *Time and Tide*, *Christmas Pie*, and *Winter Pie*.

CONTENTS

INTRODUCTION
BY
MALCOLM MUGGERIDGE

THE first Nicolas Bentley drawings I ever saw were his illustrations in Hugh Kingsmill's delightful anthology, *The Worst of Love*. This was a long time ago, and ever since I have greatly admired his work. There is, about his drawing and his wit, a sharpness and a neatness which I find particularly appealing. His versatility is astonishing. He writes, draws, and versifies with equal accomplishment, and still finds time to be a publisher, as well as a most charming and stimulating companion.

Like all humorists he has manias, which readers of this latest collection of his work will soon detect. Nuns, for instance. They crop up again and again, and always, to me, irresistibly. Incidentally, I have found them much appreciated in religious houses. It is a most foolish misunderstanding to suppose that there is anything irreligious in giving expression to the element of the grotesque which the outward face of piety necessarily comprehends. There is no sacrilege in the inclusion of gargoyles in the structure of medieval cathedrals. Only the irreligious wish to protect the institutional manifestations of religion from ridicule. Blasphemy, like pornography, is abysmally unfunny; and to the truly religious, laughter, however directed, is always blessed.

Bentley is, of course, a satirist. *How Can You Bear to be Human?* is no rhetorical question. It is seriously posed. And, after all, how can we? A quick glance round might easily evoke the answer so forcefully presented by Swift in Gulliver's fourth voyage – that we can't, and would prefer to be horses. This, however, leaves humour out of account. Man, I understand, is the only creature on this earth known to laugh. Laughter is the mark of belonging to *homo sapiens*. Bentley

9

therefore, in making us laugh, answers his own question. We can bear to be human because, as humans, we can laugh.

It is true that the laughter induced by Bentley is often wry. 'The Earl and Countess of Kilkenny, and no laughter, please', and 'Dr Hoffmeyer is *absolutely* brilliant', are good examples. So is 'Kiss me, Hardy'. His character studies in 'Historic Moment' and 'Strange Interlude', for instance, have a decidedly acidic flavour. This, however, does not mean they are cruel, but rather that, like a good Martini, they are dry. Humour cannot be painless. It is a stimulant, not a sedative. There is all the difference in the world between Don Quixote and Christopher Robin.

Bentley, then, to be appreciated, must be taken as he is. If he finds something hilarious in an execution it is not because he thinks it funny that a man's head should be cut off. On the contrary, there is compassion in realizing that even the appalling cruelties in which human beings indulge convey that vast chasm between human aspiration and human performance from which all authentic humour derives. As a matter of fact, humorists have, for the most part, exceptionally compassionate natures. Bentley certainly has. *How Can You Bear to be Human?*, as I have said, tells us how we can, and must, bear it – with a smile.

Strange Interlude

HER dress was of black velvet and severely plain in the medieval style, fitting close to the trunk, which was well packed and with a waist somewhere in the region of the pelvis. The tight sleeves tapered to a point over the back of the hand and the full-gathered skirt fell just short of the ankles. These, to my faint surprise, were hidden in white open-work stockings and the feet in good Cromwellian shoes with square buckles. This was evening dress, and, as evening dress calls for jewellery, a locket on a black ribbon was tied tight round the column of her throat and a string of chunky amber beads, like the teeth of a chain-smoking dinosaur, hung down below her midriff. Amber, too, was pendent from her lobes, which peeped out from under a pair of coiled and greying plaits. Her face reminded me of, among other things, a self-portrait by Hokusai, except that her small elongated eyes were further diminished by pale horn-rimmed glasses.

'How do you do?' she said as we were introduced, with a grave articulation that made it sound as though she really wanted to know. I having asked the same of her, it began to look as though conversation had lagged beyond hope of recovery. But no such luck.

'You have tried the punch, I presume?' she said presently, in the tones of one who would take no denial. I tried to laugh off the beaker of whisky in my hand with some feeble theorizing about herbs and spices not being good for the old digestion.

She looked at me like a disapproving musk rat. A moment's thought would have told me there wasn't anything I could teach her about the properties of herbs and spices, or, I suspected, about gillyflower water, the making of rush mats, pomanders, or how to vamp an accompaniment on the bass viol.

'This yours?'

And so the talk slid over to other things. We spoke of her habitat. It seemed she had her being, if you could call it that, in a small Buckinghamshire town, which on that account alone would no doubt prefer to be nameless. I knew, because it was a household word where words now obsolete and of Saxon origin are the common currency of speech, that she and her husband did very nicely thank you out of a craft factory, where they turned out textiles of plain but mediocre design and furniture of more than mediocre discomfort. I glanced at her capable hand, with its heavy cornelian ring, as she raised it to remove with charming unselfconsciousness a hair that had got into her mouth, and I imagined it, shuttle-clasped, moving with dexterous speed between warp and woof as her loom exuded some hideous fabric.

Now to her side came the diffident bulk of her mate, looking as uncomfortable as a plucked ostrich in his unaccustomed evening togs. A fellow who couldn't let ill alone, he had added to his troubles by wearing a black stock that pushed his hair up at the back into a fringe like Grock's wig. For what seemed longer no doubt than it was they looked at each other speech-lessly in mutual satisfaction. Presently this period of silent adoration came to an end, and in a voice higher than the chandelier her spouse gave tongue.

'Well, my deahr?'

To which, in tones somewhat lower than his, she flashed the riposte:

'Well?'

Again silence fell between them and they stood smiling mutely at each other.

'You have tried the punch?' she said at last.

Unable to block my ears in time, I caught his shrill response.

'I have indeed and I pronounce it capital.'

He grinned at me shyly with teeth that were rather too far apart. I noticed his hand had been surreptitiously exploring his pocket, and I guessed what for. He leant towards me and said *sotto voce*, with a look that appealed for my support and failed utterly:

'Do you suppose our hostess would permit a pipe?'

'I don't smoke, so I wouldn't know,' I said, lapsing through sheer nerves into the affectation of the conditional. He peered about him with a look of wildly exaggerated consternation and then, in order, I suppose, to keep up the conspiratorial pretence, tiptoed away.

Once more the colourless almond eyes of my companion – how else to describe her? – watched me with unblinking expectancy. I felt I could not disappoint her. After all she was, or appeared to be, a woman. It was unfortunate; my knowledge of how to make a rush mat had deserted me with startling suddenness as soon as I left my kindergarten. And what did I know of the bass viol? I tried to rack my brains for the latest intelligence from the Dolmetsch front, but they refused to be racked. Finally, for want of a better utterance, I found myself telling her that I had just come back from Wembley.

'Wembley,' she said. Her tone was that of the Blessèd Damozel, a tone of sweet, incurious surprise.

'Trinder on ice,' I said, 'or rather, Aladdin.'

Through closed lips she made a sound like that of someone playing a one-stringed fiddle with an empty bottle. As luck would have it, and a better stroke seldom came my way, her hero at this moment returned. His pipe was in his hand and I was sorry to see that his manner was that of one who has glad tidings to impart.

'Deahr,' said he, 'a surprise: Amanda has brought her lute and is going to sing.'

Whereunto answereth his ladye with tranquil mien, yet merrily withal, 'O joy!'

The Mystery of Napoleon's Hat

MANY reasons have been put forward to account for Napoleon's fame, apart from those put forward by Napoleon himself. Historians, politicians, novelists, and film directors seem never tired of airing their theories about the small corporal. But I know of no theory that takes into account the importance of the Emperor's hat.

Imagine, for instance, how different things might have been at Jena or Marengo with Napoleon in a white topper, such as was fashionable at the time, the crown being rather larger at the top than at the base. Imagine the effect, especially on Josephine, of a small sugar-loaf hat surmounting that dumpy imperial figure. Imagine the Emperor at Austerlitz, with the plumed casque of a French dragoon coming well down over his ears. Imagine a flat *tricorne* precariously balanced on that rounded pate, so that a sharp turn of the head must have left the hat facing towards the front.

The fate of nations cannot be sealed by a man whose hat causes the bystanders to grin, and Napoleon knew this. Whereas Fox, for example, did not. Though his vast beaver effectively hid most of the Opposition from view, it still left the Government's supporters something to laugh at. In a topper of more modest proportions, who knows to what heights Fox might not have risen?

Napoleon's genius showed itself in an astonishing variety of ways. It was apparent not only in war and in diplomacy, but also in the art of good government, in his judgement of men, and still more in his judgement of moments. Above all, it was shown in his choice of a hat.

Many famous men have been distinguished by slight idiosyncrasies of appearance. Some like Alma-Tadema, for instance, whose appearance was in itself unique, have been distinguished for little else. Both Solomon and Louis Quatorze were known for the glory of their apparel; Charlemagne was renowned for the length of his beard. (It was said he could kneel on it, though it is not recorded why this was necessary.) The Black Prince was famed for his funereal armour; Disraeli for his waistcoats; Gladstone not only for his collars but also for his bags; no one knew quite what it was that Clemenceau wore for a hat, but it will certainly live in the annals of history; Lloyd George had his hair bobbed; Cromwell had warts; and Keir Hardie wore a tweed cap. But a tweed cap, even though a contemporary photograph shows it to have had a retractable undercarriage which fastened on top with a piece of string, is not, for sheer *étalage*, in the same class as Napoleon's hat.

'Say "How d'you do?"'

17

The principle on which this singular head-piece was designed is said to be a mystery even to the most redoubtable and experienced hatters. It is not known, for instance, whether, as some surmise, the back could be let down to facilitate the heaving of coal, or whether the front could be folded up to form the thing into a watering can. Its possibilities as a muffin dish, a font, and an umbrella-stand have also been canvassed from time to time by interested parties. Indeed, the infinite possibilities of such a hat could hardly fail to stir a practical imagination.

In the museum at Boulogne there used to be a hat that was treasured as a genuine Napoleonic relic. I saw it once and was immediately impressed not only by its shape but by its size. It was enormous, and looking at it, I was reminded of Chesterton's lines addressed to my father:

We wore one hat, smoked one cigar,
One standing at each end.

Certainly there was room for at least two under this saucepanlike covering. Yet there is no record, so far as I know, that the Emperor ever suffered – except perhaps in a metaphorical sense – from a swelled head. I am therefore puzzled to know what went on inside that part of the hat that was not filled by the imperial cranium. Was it stuffed with dispatches from the battlefield?

18

'*Look – Ivy Compton-Burnett.*'

Or with old newspapers? Or was there a tea-cosy inside it as a lining? Did it perhaps contain a secret drawer for Josephine's letters? Or was there a packet of sandwiches there and a flask of cognac for sudden emergencies?

That there must have been more in it than met the eye seems certain, or how else could the little chap have kept the thing aloft? For on anyone with a head of even medium size it must have fallen about the shoulders like a cape.

The possibility of supernatural means should not be ruled out. Levitation may be laughed at, and there are some mediums who invite a sceptical smile even when in an upright position, but the power of some such unknown agency would still have its uses. The raising of the hat to ladies, for instance, might well be worked on the same principle, if it could only be discovered, and would be certain to give innocent amusement to passers-by.

Napoleon's consciousness of his appearance was not merely a sign of vanity. His cultivation of the picturesque was not simply to gratify a whim. Like most successful men of blood and iron, with the possible exception of Bismarck, whose personality could have charmed only another walrus, Napoleon knew that to appeal to the people you must appeal first of all to their imagination. Appeals to reason or to sacrifice could be made with far greater certainty of response when the public held in its mind's eye the vision of a leader who seemed at once romantic, masterful, splendid, and mysterious. This is no doubt the real reason for the milk-white steed, the ineradicable frown, the retinue of picturesque generals, the silences and sudden storms, the studied air of abstraction, and, of course, the hat.

In the matter of dress some men are a law unto themselves, and Napoleon's sartorial sense was always unorthodox. The

'*I want some material for an iron curtain.*'

20

'Look, lady – it's you, honest!'

uniform of the First Consul was slightly bizarre, though not lacking in chic. The coronation robes, too, were of original design. In dressing to please oneself, whether by imitating the fastidiousness of Brummell or the knickerbockery of Bernard Shaw, a man's clothes became so much a part of his personality that it is difficult to imagine him in any other sort of garb. Napoleon created for himself an outfit which it is impossible to imagine anyone else wearing. Who but he could have got into – or got out of – that bottle-green cut-away, so queerly fashioned, so intricately buttoned? Who but he could have worn the hat? Even Hitler, who seemed to fancy some affinity with the Emperor, stuck to his own ill-designed get-up. And was ever a man so lacking in a sense of dress? It was lucky for us perhaps that in Sir Winston Churchill we had a leader who knew from experience the parts that a hat may play in history.

On Bathing and Beards

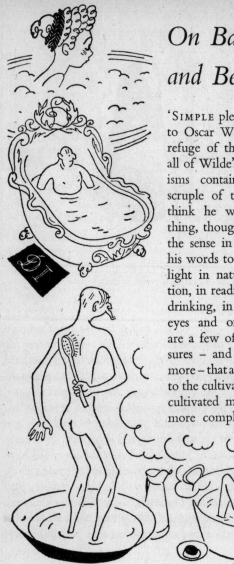

'SIMPLE pleasures,' according to Oscar Wilde, 'are the last refuge of the complex.' Not all of Wilde's so-called aphorisms contain more than a scruple of truth, but here I think he was on to something, though not precisely in the sense in which he meant his words to be accepted. Delight in nature, in conversation, in reading, in eating and drinking, in the use of one's eyes and one's imagination, are a few of the simple pleasures – and there are many more – that appeal most readily to the cultivated man; and the cultivated man is *ipso facto* a more complex one than the philistine. Few of the pleasures that the philistine enjoys are not complicated by considerations of gain, rivalry, or expense, or else by rituals, rules, or regulations.

Wilde goes too far perhaps in describing simple pleasures as the last refuge of his kind (for what a Freudian cat's cradle was there!) but they certainly come well up on my own list; and simpleton though I may be compared to, say, Professor Bronowski, compared to the man who delights more in Wolverhampton Wanderers than in Wordsworth, I am a creature of infinite complexity, hence my enjoyment of the simpler forms of pleasure. I know of few, for instance, to equal that of lying in warm water. The lascivious Poppaea, so they say, bathed in asses' milk (and what could have been more appropriate for anyone who was fool enough to fall for Nero?) but I doubt whether she enjoyed lying in her milky tub more than I in my plain warm water.

This is one of the few simple pleasures that are perhaps shared equally by the complex and the uncomplex, that is enjoyed both by the great and by the humble. Among the great, for instance, there is my wife (nine stone six in her nylons) and also Mr Cyril Connolly, who could hardly be much less in his. 'Both my happiness and my unhappiness,' he says, 'I owe to the love of pleasure' – and was ever a truer word said about any of us? – and enumerates among his own, 'lying in warm water'. Then there was the Emperor Diocletian, and Lord Rokeby, brother of 'Fidget' Montague. Upon all of them water has exerted an irresistible attraction.

The case of Lord Rokeby – and he *was* a case, if ever I heard of one – is less well known than I think it deserves to be. I hold no brief for eccentricity in itself, which begins so often in a desire to attract admiration and usually ends so sadly in having the opposite effect. But from eccentricity carried as far as Lord Rokeby carried it, which must have been about as far as it would stretch, I feel there is a moral to be drawn, as from all extremes, and it is probably that cleanliness is next to Godliness.

England has always been a rare place for eccentrics, and Lord Rokeby must surely be one of its rarest. He was among other things a naturalist, perhaps the original of Edward Lear's Old Man with a Beard – and spent a good deal of time watching the antics of other odd birds. So great, indeed, was his love of nature that he could not abide to have his beard tampered with. Consequently he allowed it the uninterrupted freedom of the house, so that it came in time to be as large, if not as useful, as a doormat.

But in his love of immersion Lord Rokeby went to even further lengths. Once in the sea, he would stay there till he fainted away and had to be dragged out by main force. In order, no doubt, to prolong life, he eventually built himself a bath in which he sat, decently submerged, receiving his friends and eating his meals off a floating platter.

Seeing that he allowed the water to be warmed only by such heat as nature provided, you might suppose that his constitution would not long have withstood the strain he put upon it, what with constant immersion and the weight of his beard, not to mention the claims of society and conscience, for he was active both in political and religious matters and would not allow even his aquatic passion to interfere with either of these interests. Yet in spite of everything he lasted till he was nearly ninety, by which time his beard had become the pride of the county. Where, I wonder, will Mr Connolly's beard have got to, or my wife's, for that matter, by the time they are ninety?

If reason still holds sway I feel pretty sure that I at that age will still present, to

'*Father, I want you to meet Mother.*'

24

anyone who can take it, the same gaunt smooth-shaven pan that has sent me reeling back from the mirror with a groan every morning for the past forty years or so. Yet time was when vanity (for I cannot imagine what else can have persuaded me to such folly) helped me to sport a growth on my upper lip that would have done credit to the most imbecile member of the Handlebars Club.

In the days of D'Orsay it was possible for a man to train his whiskers like a creeping vine about his cheek without being thought to look a fool. But man's appearance has grown so penny-plain that simpler specimens, having no other attributes worthy of interest, now feel they must claim attention by the size and unruly behaviour of their moustaches. A good, honest, work-a-day moustache, like Earl Attlee's, for instance, can be, if not a thing of beauty and a joy forever to Countess Attlee, at least a thing of sterling worth, and if left untrimmed, a useful aid against minestrone.

Any man, whatever his age, who has a mind to set about growing whiskers, should see that they are trained to the house, and not such as will catch in the banisters or set fire to the face if exposed near a naked flame, or, worse still, look as though you have tried to brush a streak of soot from under your nose.

Above all, do not try to grow whiskers too soon. Although the spirit may be willing, you will find that the flesh is weak. Down is no substitute for bristles. Remember Cressida's indictment of Troilus: 'Alas, poor chin! many a wart is richer.'

25

'*When I was a spiv there wasn't such things as teddy boys.*'

Cecil B. de Mille

Cecil B. de Mille,
Rather against his will,
Was persuaded to leave Moses
Out of *The Wars of the Roses*.

'*Mother, this is the Chief of my department.*'

Mechanical Problem

How many revs a minute
Would Ruskin turn in his grave
If he'd seen that exhibition
That Salvador Dali gave?

Historic Moment

WE were sitting so that we faced each other across the table. He was a Cambridge man, name of Cedric Cudham, a minor don. He had a florid face and a hairy neck and his eyes were small and myopic. He was full of history and had that air of invincible superiority that is so often a sign of a second-class intellect. At forty-odd he still retained some of the deliberate gaucheries of the undergraduate – there was a bright bandanna handkerchief sticking out of the pocket of his dinner jacket – only now they had become the deliberate eccentricities of a conceited chump. He spoke quickly and authoritatively in a harsh voice that cut through conversation like a buzz-saw. He was every inch a don, of the crass, self-opinionated type, and with each mouthful of the soufflé that he shovelled in (his table manners were none too good) I longed to kick his teeth in. He had a good strong set and I could imagine a heavy briar clamped between them as he sprawled in his airless rooms scribbling away at some erudite paper on the Diet of Worms.

They had put him next to a healthy-looking girl called Myrtle, who in some strange way managed to give an impression of chic and yet remained unquestionably English. With what intention they had been paired off it was hard to say. Clearly he hadn't much interest in women of later date than Madame de Maintenon or with less political acumen than she must have had. Myrtle looked as though her political acumen began and ended with the knowledge that Daddy always votes Conservative.

Having listened with a slightly dazed expression to a short lecture on Napoleon's strategy at Austerlitz, Myrtle deemed it the right moment to shove in her tiny oar.

'I thought Marlon Brando was awfully like him in *Désirée*, didn't you?'

'Why, Dad, I didn't know you could rock an' roll!'

'Don't it seem silly, eh? workin' at a bank on a Bank 'oliday.'

'Who is Marlon Brando?'

It was just a little too brusque. A lesser fool than Cedric would have seen how far calculated indifference towards a girl like Myrtle could be carried without giving her the needle. This time she felt it.

'Oh, Mr Cudham, surely you *must* have heard of Marlon Brando?'

'Must I?'

'Oh, well, I mean – well, one must be rather an oyster in a cloister not to.'

She knew exactly how to swing it and did so with a sweet reasonableness that took the blunt edge off but made the point a little sharper.

'He was absolutely Napoleon,' she said. 'I mean, he really was, really. Oh, he was wonderful!'

'You are alluding now to Napoleon?'

Myrtle – and I don't wonder – seemed rooted for the moment by this shaft of academic irony.

'*Not* to Napoleon. The only thing I know about him is that ludicrous hat.'

'He did possess other attributes, of course,' said Cedric, dry as ginger ale, though not as sparkling.

'Yes, but actually this film's all about his sex life.'

'I'm afraid I don't often go to Hollywood films,' Cedric said. His tone put Hollywood, and in fact the whole industry, exactly where it belonged – beyond the pale.

'Oh, do tell us, what *do* you go to?'

Myrtle, in spite of appearances, seemed to be nobody's fool, but she knew somebody else's when she saw one, and at twenty paces a blind man could have spotted Cedric as being Acton's or Macaulay's or in fact the dumb disciple of any

Robert Browning at work

historical sage who had been dead long enough not to offer any competition.

'You adhere to the concept of perpetual motion, Miss Hesketh, like a good many of your generation, if I may say so.'

Myrtle rolled a round and startled eye in my direction.

'But *do* say so. Or does that mean something I oughtn't to know about?'

'*That's okay, Miss Matson, we know how they sing it at the Condor Club.*'

'The desire for movement *per se*, or shall I say the desire for what they call in the United States "going places", doesn't necessarily exert an equal attraction upon succeeding generations. You "go" to the cinema; I "go" – at least, in so far as I may be said to "go" anywhere – in pursuit of the University beagles.'

He gave a broad, bland, and rather fleeting smile to show that (*a*) as she wasn't worth more than a moment's consideration he bore her no rancour, and (*b*) the subject was now closed.

'Is that fun?' The flat innocency of Myrtle's tone seemed to imply that of all sports none sounded more of a deadly bore than beagling.

'Indeed it is. And it is also a considerable test of stamina.'

'You should come with me some time, Cudham,' I said, 'on the Monte Carlo rally. That's a pretty good test of stamina. You'd enjoy it.'

He turned his tight-lipped smile on me and his little eyes glittered behind their heavy lenses.

'Would I? I doubt whether you would, though.'

He was wrong there. I know what those ice-covered bends are like going over the Col du Fau. In a low-slung sports job like the one I drove in '54, and given a patch of mist, with him on the outside edge it would have been money for old rope.

'What's wrong with the cinema, though, Mr Cudham?' Myrtle wasn't going to let him get away with it.

'What indeed?'

'Well, for my money,' I said, 'there's Hollywood.'

Myrtle looked faintly disappointed.

'I thought you were batting on my side,' she said.

'Well, yes, but I'm against vesting authority in the lower apes.'

'Our friend has put it in a nutshell,' Cedric said, smug as a bishop. I didn't care for our being classed as friends, but I let it ride.

'Well, I don't care what you say,' Myrtle said brightly, 'I think *Désirée*'s a jolly good film and I adore Marlon Brando.'

'*Chacun à son goût*,' said Cedric with a hint of a shrug, just to show there was some Gallic blood as well as soda water in his veins, at the same time watching me to see whether I appreciated how delicate was his irony.

'Well, what's your taste like then, Mr Cudham?'

'In what?'

'I mean in film stars.'

'Well, I've told you, I seldom go –'

'Oh, yes. But I bet I know exactly the type of woman who attracts you, Mr Cudham.'

He tried a deprecating snigger which didn't quite come off.

'Then I congratulate you on your percipience,' he said.

We seemed to be swinging well outside his conversational orbit, which I've no doubt left the relationship of the sexes where it was when Herbert Spencer fell over it. But the man's vanity was too strong for him; he stuck his neck out a little further.

'For example?'

'Oh, well, someone like Marilyn Monroe probably,' said Myrtle.

Cedric sniggered again. Then the prig in him, never very far from the surface, came to the top and leant over.

'And would you mind also telling me who your tailor is?'

'I don't think Miss Monroe and I would have much to say to each other.'

'That would be one time, Mr Cudham,' said Myrtle, 'when what you would have to say wouldn't matter.'

'*I like to have it on for* Music While You Work.'

Some Early Experiments with Horseless Carriages

ONE of the earliest desires that I can remember was for some form – I wasn't particular in those days about which form – of artificial locomotion. That desire is still with me, and as my gait returns with the years to that erratic waddle that marked my first attempts to walk, so it increases.

My first locomotive was a flat-chested woman in a starched apron. She was called Nanny Pooke and all that I know about her derives from a faded photograph showing her sitting rather unsuitably dressed on a broiling beach.

My second locomotive must have been a pram, probably one with a semi-elliptical basket-work body slung high on a high narrow chassis and with some damn fool parasol arrangement sticking up on a rod at the back. Imagine, if you can bear to, the spectacle I must have presented, as of a Dutch cheese wrapped in a pelisse of oyster-coloured satin and topped with a starched tam o'shanter two feet wide.

Next came a push-chair, which I hated, though not as much as I hated walking. Later on I recollect being moved from place to place by horse-drawn transport. The internal combustion engine having made its regrettable entry into society only a year or so before I made mine, the hansom cab and the horse bus were still making their leisurely way about the streets. Indeed, the London taxi-cab and I made our débuts almost simultaneously.

If memory serves aright, one of the last horse buses to ply for hire in London was a creaking snail of a thing painted blue and white which used to totter from the Pole Star near Swiss Cottage to some hinterland beyond the Spaniards' Inn on Hampstead Heath. It sounds a romantic journey – from the

Pole Star to the Spaniards' Inn, where legend has lodged Dick Turpin. In fact, all I can remember of it was an effluvium of booze from the ancient conductor, and the brown bowler-hatted driver whipping off small boys who tried to cling to the backstairs advertisements of Jeyes' Fluid and Pears' Soap.

In due course I graduated to the dignity of a scooter and later to roller skates. This was a perilous period, for anyone in the line of my trajectory, as well as for me. At the beginning mine were usually the limbs that suffered most. But as I grew emboldened by experience, my speed increased, but not, unfortunately, mastery of the fatal footwear. To accept an invitation to accompany me for an afternoon at the skating rink was to accept, if not the kiss of death, at least the risk of grave and life-long disfigurement. Even the instructors used to give me a wide berth, though sometimes it was not wide enough.

There was one splendid individual who used to be got up in the quaint semblance of a Muscovite, wearing a cap like an astrakhan tea-cosy ornamented with an aigrette. One afternoon, as I was hurtling round the rink, I inadvertently swept his legs from under him, while he in turn brought down a pair of nervous beginners in the path of some rather racy characters going round hell for leather. In a matter of seconds the rink was piled high with human debris, and the following morning my father received a note from the manager seeking his cooperation in placing a permanent ban on my attendance.

Parental fears, whether for my own incompetence or that of others I don't know, forbade the bicycle. I was thirty-five before I got one and by then the first flush of youthful ecstasy that comes with mastery of the bicycle didn't rise to my cheeks as spontaneously as if I had been a year or two younger. Besides, I had already owned motor-cars by that time.

My first car was in many ways the most satisfactory I ever possessed. It had no engine. Its power was derived from a simple pedal-and-chain arrangement, and when the chain came off it was easy enough to put it back again. To one whose knowledge of mechanical processes is limited, this is an advantage. What induces my car to go, or what more often fails to induce it to go, I have never thought it prudent to ask. It isn't that I don't like to expose my ignorance: it exposes itself. But as there is usually somebody at hand with an astute mechanical mind and grubby fingers who can tell what is wrong in a trice, I feel it safer to leave my troubles in the hands of these good Samaritans.

The only things that ever went wrong with my pedal-and-chain model were that the steering wheel sometimes came off, and once, when the car was getting on in years, the back seat fell out. Since I was sitting on it at the time, I too made an involuntary exit, leaving the car to trundle towards a lady who was looking into a shop window. It caught her behind the knees and she sat down precipitately on the bonnet of the car.

Being a lady of substantial build, it was her dignity that suffered more than anything else, except the car, which looked as though it had been passed through a rolling mill.

Perhaps it was this incident that gave me an ineradicable dislike of motor-cars. I admit their convenience but I seldom travel in one without reflecting how much pleasanter it must have been to travel in a chaise. Doctor Johnson, who, in spite of his irascibility and unprepossessing appearance, now and then assumed the airs of a gallant, held that human happiness consisted in driving in a chaise with a pretty woman. And who am I to dispute with Doctor Johnson when men of learning and profundity had their ears chewed off merely for making some innocent comment? Although travelling in the eighteenth century must often have been hazardous and uncomfortable, at least it was leisurely, and the absence of leisure is what I regret most about the motor-car. Speed has never had for me the attraction that it undoubtedly has for many people.

The only car I have ever driven that was really leisurely was the first one I bought, and that was about twenty years ago. It was so goddamned leisurely that you could hardly get it to move at all. It was described when I bought it as second-hand. I didn't know, until I had driven it away, that the hands through which it had passed must have been those of an orang-outang; and no ordinary orang-outang either, but one of exceptional strength and impatience.

At the end of three weeks I found some imbecile with just enough nous to have diddled the driving-test inspector, and he bought the thing for a song. I would have sold it for the opening bars alone, but as money seemed no object to this fool, I felt it was really doing a kindness to take some off him and so prevent his frittering it away.

The next car I bought was a honey. I might have had it still if it hadn't been for the war. But then I might have had a lot of things if it hadn't been for the war. I might have had a

'Good Lord, we forgot the onions!'

steady income, a good appetite, and general feeling of healthy well-being. But on the whole, being the muggins that I am about what goes on under a bonnet, except possibly that of a Salvation Army lass, the advantages of a car that doesn't go wrong probably outweigh those of a good appetite, a healthy mind in a healthy body, possibly even of a steady income.

To some this may seem a worldly and unethical attitude. But then we live in a worldly and unethical age – witness the Church of England as a landlord – and I speak only as a child of my times when I say that a car that works seems preferable to a conscience that doesn't. I know, because I once had a conscience that did and I still have a car that doesn't.

That I shall one day have a really magnificent car, as well as a steadier income, a better appetite, and all the rest of it, is among my fondest wishes. But he who dwells perpetually in the shadow of Carey Street cannot be the arbiter of his own fate; a painful truth to which I reconciled myself a long time ago. The prospect of getting a new car of any kind, let alone the sleek, white-walled, chromium-plated, supercharged colossus with which my fancy toys after reading the advertisements, is fading with the years. It looks as though I shall end my career as a motorist with another pedal-and-chain model. At least I shall know then what to do if anything goes wrong.

NICOLAS
BENTLEY

'*I can't think why you don't wear contact lenses.*'

'And I honestly wouldn't spend another winter in England, if I were you.'

Standing Room Only

When I was a boy I was brought up to act in a way that most young men – and I regret to say a good many of their elders – now seem to think rather absurd. I was taught that it was polite to give my seat to a lady if she should happen to be standing in a bus or a train. It was a common courtesy among men of all classes, and the offer likewise went to ladies of every shape and size, irrespective of age, income group, creed, colour, or professional status. Many are the seats I have warmed in my time, for the well-born as well as for the ill-favoured.

There was a nun, for instance, of the Carmelite Order, to whom I remember offering my seat in a Hornsey tram – though what I was doing going to Hornsey I can't imagine, for I was a gently nurtured boy. But there I was, so up I got and doffed my hideous little cap to the Mother Superior. She must have taken a rather literal view of her office, I think, for she said nothing but gave me a jagged little smile and planked herself down on my sherbet sucker, which I had been too slow and too shy to retrieve. I can still see her, after she had left the bus, a stately figure moving down Hornsey Rise with a pink paper bag sticking to the posterior folds of her medieval gown.

That was long ago, but I fancy that ever since there has been a kind of conspiracy among nuns to avoid travelling in the vehicles in which I travel. Perhaps the incident got bruited about in the convents; at any rate, I have never again met so much as a novitiate to whom I could offer my seat.

Nowadays, especially in the rush hour, a woman must be more nimble than any man ahead of her if she wants to make sure of a seat. She must be able to out-stare, out-jostle, and if necessary, out-rage the rudest of them if she wishes to seize that which once would have been regarded as hers merely by virtue of her sex.

What is it that has brought about this change, this decay in courtesy? A more cynical character than I might suggest that women have only themselves to blame. It was not men, after all, who first demanded equal recognition of the sexes. That demand came from women, and was soon – and inevitably – followed by the assertion of other rights and freedoms. Of course, the rot must have set in a long time ago, probably in pre-history days. Neanderthal Man was no doubt as much under the thumb of Neanderthal Woman as you or I under that of her twentieth-century counterpart.

Yet on the whole I am very glad that the women who demand equality have got what they wanted, though I suspect that some of them must occasionally feel it is rather more than they bargained for. I am old-fashioned enough to think that equality of the sexes can be carried too far. I am all for women doctors, women architects, women actuaries, women bi-metallists, women acrobats, women in the armed services, and so forth. I think it is an excellent thing that they should belong to Parliament, to trades unions, and to learned bodies; that they should vote and smoke and drive cars, provided that they do so from the front seat. I see no objection to their wearing trousers – in the literal sense – and within a reasonable span of hip. In fact, I think it is a good thing that they should do most of the things that men do: but they should not expect – nor be expected – to be treated as their equals in every sphere.

They should not be bishops, for instance, nor indeed preachers of any sect; already on public platforms there are enough bores among the male sex. Women should not be lawyers or bookies either, for they are required to rant for their living, and a woman who rants deserves what is usually the lot of a ranting female. Women should not box, as some do in France, nor wrestle, as in America. They should not spit or swear, or imitate the appearance of the male, although a tweed cap secured with a hatpin, such as it was not uncommon to see when I was a boy, gave ladies of the working class a characteristic touch that I was rather fond of. Above all, women should not imitate, or seek to share, the camaraderie of men among men, which is sometimes barely tolerable even among one's intimate friends. With an alcoholic effort and at rare intervals it may be allowed in certain other coteries, such as among rotarians, Old Boys, commercial travellers, and the like, who are forced by circumstances into a state of deter-mined jollity. But back-slapping, or its equivalent among ladies, and the tedious toasting of 'absent friends', not to men-tion the swapping of yarns, is so mortifying an experience that any decent woman must instinctively recoil from it as would a Baptist from the Pope.

By overstepping the mark in trying to assert such rights, and by attempting to establish an illogical equality of be-haviour, women sometimes do their sex a disservice. It was not for the right merely to ape men's manners that Mrs Pank-hurst assumed the sacrificial padlock, nor that Mrs Despard determined that the policeman's lot should be, if possible, a far from happy one. The fundamentals of good manners do not alter; as Goethe pointed out, good manners are founded on the society of women and are therefore ageless.

In this rather old-fashioned belief, and at the risk of seeming ridiculous to most of my fellow men, I shall continue to rise whenever necessary and offer my seat to ladies as long as my limbs will support me.

Diana Dors

49

'The Earl and Countess of Kilkenny, and no laughter, please.'

Ambassador Extraordinary

So this was her, the fabulous Mrs Lois Everett Schuyler, and I use the word fabulous advisedly. If everything she had been credited with was true, her career – begun, so says the voice of history sounding through the columns of *Time*, on the wrong side of the tracks in Cleveland, Ohio – if it was all true, her career makes that of the du Barry sound like the guileless existence of a suburban *Hausfrau*.

And here she was, in the Ladies' Annexe of the Athenaeum; which, to some of her kind, if such there be, might seem their apotheosis; but not to Lois Schuyler. Whispers from Washington already spoke of her, her Episcopalian birth notwithstanding, as the President's (unofficial) representative at the Vatican. For having in her time espoused or embraced a variety of causes, faiths, principles, opinions, and nuptial partners, few of them compatible with each other, she could take a conversion to Rome in her stride.

Not that that slow, undulating shamble of hers could be properly called a stride. Still, it does serve to get her from place to place, if not always on time. But for the ever-busy, time, if it doesn't exactly stand still, seems to slow down to an easy dog-trot. How else would Lois ever get through her daily time-table? Those *tête-à-tête* breakfasts in Downing Street; those luncheons in Paris with NATO's top brass; those drinks – straight tomato juice these days, for behind the inevitable dark glasses Lois has a sharp eye for the interest value of unorthodox virtues – the drinks, then, with some visiting celebrity from the old country, Harold Stassen perhaps, or Danny, or Henry Luce, or maybe some Olympian waif like Truman Capote; and then home – home for a quiet evening with just the telephone, the typewriter, and the tape-recorder.

Home at the moment is a little gem just not too far from

Claridge's, and on it Lois, with the willing help of a young man who runs a decorator's business from his mummy's flat in Lowndes Square, has lavished all that alimony can buy. The rooms are rather small perhaps and seem a little overcrowded, but the place has been done over in exquisite taste, so who cares? Not Lois. Hollywood-Florentine, like it was in the apartment she had on Beekman Place, would have been all right with her, only Simon absolutely would not *allow* any indoor ironwork, and Simon has such perfectly wonderful taste. And taste, as Picasso told Lois one night at the Marquis de Cuevas', is turribly, turribly important.

So there she is, the enigmatic, discreetly famed Lois, sitting with us in the Ladies' Annexe, the tiny insignia of the Legion of Honour (*cinquième classe*) in her lapel, the aroma of her 'Miss Dior' mingling with the smoke of our cigar. And it's half past nine and you wonder how she ever finds time to write all the things she writes, those dispatches for the President, those articles for *Collier's*, those features for *Life* (Mrs Pandit Nehru – India's Woman of Destiny), those broadcasts, those endorsements for the safety and comfort of this airline or that, those sharp-etched *contes*, to one of which Edmund Wilson once referred in the mistaken belief that it was by someone else. How does she manage it? No one quite seems to know, but somehow she gets through it all.

Under the tousled chic of that tiger-tawny mop there is a mind precise, determined, energetic, canny, and impervious to the slings and arrows of outrageous gossip. Was it true that she started life in a honky-tonk? Could be. Those legs, that figure, still give promise, though Lois is still enough of a liddle gurrl at heart for her promises, when it's convenient, to be like pie crust; which to do her justice is maybe why she seldom makes them: she doesn't like to disappoint. And men are so foolish, so indiscreet, so possessive, so tiresomely insistent.

But men, except for Presidents, *éminences grises*, philosophical dons, and expatriate authors, bore Lois. Men are something she has had altogether too much of. Though she got along tolerably well with her first three husbands – two she divorced for natural causes, and another in a moment of sanity threw himself from the Rockefeller Centre – Larry, No. 4, was a no-good playboy. And a no-good playboy may be all you require if you're an ice-blonde doll with no brains above your hips, but is definitely not the sort of thing you want to have around if you are settling the fate of empires. As Lois told Colonel Nasser when last they met – she was stopping off at Cairo on the way back from a quick trip to her old, old friend and saint, Schweitzer – as she said to Colonel Nasser, 'Well, you know what de Tockveel said, don't you? You *don't*? My! Well, de Tockveel said, I forget what exactly

'*Did you hear that one about the square of the hypotenuse?*'

in so many words, but it was just exactly applicable, Colonel, to this very, very tense situation that you have out here in the Middle East.'

Of course, Colonel Nasser must have felt an absolute fool, but Lois has something about her that – well, you just can't get mad at her even when you know she's right. What's the use of getting mad at a Sphinx? Except in the gravity with which they both accept the bare fact of their being, La Gioconda is more like it, for below the dark glasses plays that inscrutable smile to which have succumbed editors, psychiatrists, diplomats, head waiters, bankers, painters, commissars, cabinet ministers, and four husbands.

'How does Lois do it?' is the question that her friends ask, and her enemies, for you cannot avoid making enemies if you are engaged in making history, and can Lois help it if Fate decrees that she should usually happen to be on hand when history is giving another twist to the rack?

It must be a heartening realization for the President that in these troublous times the reputation of the United States abroad is in those capable but shapely hands – with their blood-red nails and that big *cabochon* emerald on the third finger.

'*Have I been giving it too much water, d'you think?*'

For details of
advertising in
this space
apply to
the Deanery

Charles Morgan

Lunching one day with Morgan
I was weary and ill at ease,
For he started quoting *Sparkenbroke*,
Before we had reached the cheese;
I knew not what he was saying
(And was past caring then),
So I struck him on the schnozzle
With the Corton, 1910.

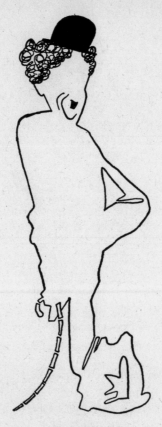

Charlie Chaplin

Harry's

THAT'S him, the one in the white overall, with the oyster satin tie and the crisp, refined accent. That wide white smile that curves off the upper lip and then stops dead, don't let that fool you; it's strictly for the customers. I guess he hasn't much sense of humour, not about himself anyway. Looks like a big baby's, that pink, chubby face, with those honey-brown eyes; a baby with a slightly broken nose; and if it weren't for that load of grease on the kinky hair you could see that it's sort of reddish.

'What's it to be, gent'emen? There's some very, very nice beef today, yes? Okay – two chopped livers, two lemon teas. Any *lutkas* with the beef? And a cucumber? Okay.'

Wish I could speak as fast sometimes. Says twice as much in half the time and no words wasted. Pleasantries are not for him, nor for the customers. Business is business and sentiment something you pay for at the cinema.

61

'*Lutkas!*' Get the way he leans out over the trap and bellows down into the kitchen? You'd never think that with those tones, almost mincing in their refinement, he could produce a sound so earthy. 'Somebody dead down there?' He looks at me all of a sudden. 'You come to the funeral?' The invitation's issued with that faintly menacing smile that seems about as near as he can get to overt amiability.

No stools to be had for the moment, so we take our chopped livers and stand around eating them with sliced rye. One usually stands anyway.

'Hi, Harry.'

''lo, Wolfie, 'lo, Les. Mornin', Mr Goodman. A nice plate of beef? Or some tongues? They're very, very lovely, these tongues, Mr Goodman, just like a baby's. You boys goin' to the fight tonight? Me? You bet.'

Notice the way he hangs on to the final 't'? And those elliptical vowels. All makes for dainty conversation.

I've seen Wolfie around before, and Les too, but Mr Goodman's new. He's sixty at a guess and a very sad man. For what reason one doesn't know. Maybe it's a form of vicarious anguish for the sufferings of his race; or it could be the purchase tax on all those buttons of his. Must be a big worry. To even things up he gets a kick out of dressing himself as expensively as possible. The narrow shoes are bench-made and beautiful. The soft black hat and the melton overcoat – a magnificent piece of cloth that, Mr Goodman, if you'll allow me to say so – look brand new and probably are. His nylon shirt is as the driven snow – and from Bond Street too, or my name's not Bendelbaum. A dead quiet man, you'd say, discounting the miniscule diamond in his wedding-ring and the ivory-topped cane. His conversation, such as it is, consists mostly of shrugs, little tilts of the head, and a raising of the eye-brows or a sour pursing of the lips, always with his heavy-lidded eyes half-closed. A sad man, not like Wolfie, except for the clothes.

Wolfie's clothes are new too, of course, not less expensive

and almost as discreet. But the tie, a flash-looking job rich and
Roman in design, is a give-away. Not the sort of neckwear
you'd find on such as Mr Goodman. But Wolfie, though he
doesn't know it and wouldn't thank you for telling him so, is
an extrovert. Tallish, pink-faced, jovial, with a flat-topped
head and rippling ebony curls. He wears the latest in Ameri-
can-type glasses. His voice is high and his gift of repartee
would be no disgrace in a child of seven.

'Make mine a tongue san'wich, will you, Harry? I cou'
fancy a bita tongue s'mornin'. Guess mine's wearin' out, eh?'

Nobody laughs; nobody's meant to. It's just Wolfie's irre-
pressible way. 'How's the *gefilte*, eh?'

'Wonderful,' Harry says with great earnestness. 'Such
gefilte you won't get every day, believe me. Les – *gefilte*?'

'*Gefilte* nothing.'

Les sounds pretty sore about something or other. He gener-
ally does. He'll be another Mr Goodman one of these days,

when the cynicism and the wisecracks have dried up and there's only the self-pity left, just a quiet, miserable old man with pots of money, living in a flat in Cricklewood, the only pleasures left to him a sad game of pinochle and the wearing of very, very expensive clothes. Already Les has a new bowler hat, also a new dark overcoat, new shoes, a new tie, and smells of after-shave lotion.

So here comes Morrie. Well, well, well. And Hetty with him. This is a pleasure, surely. Somehow Harry's has never been much of a place for the girls, except you have a family interest, like Rose. She's married to Harry's cousin – the other one in the white coat, standing by the cash machine – and her sister Zena. She's married to Lew – wholesale grocery, which is a big help, as you can imagine, and just to make a package deal out of it, there's Lew's brother Stan (his other sister-in-law is married to Morrie's brother) just got started in a nice line of fancy papers (bankrupt stock), so it looks like before long Harry's going to need a helluva lot of paper napkins.

Hetty's in the mink, or something like it, because Morrie's got a cousin a wholesale furrier. It's a bit of a drag, a coat like that on a girl her size wearing needle-point heels as long as her middle finger, which, to the tip of a magenta-lacquered nail, means a good four inches. The sight of her brings out a faintly nauseating gallantry in Harry and adds a little extra polish to the refinement of his accent.

'My word, Het, you lookin' kind special this morning, eh? How's tricks?'

Hetty's smile shows her top and bottom teeth at the same time. She's as pretty as they come, but they don't come for long, not her sort. She's twenty-seven if she's a day and already her charms are a little overripe. However, Morrie's still as pleased as Punch to have her around and handles her with a proprietary delicacy that his father must have picked up from seeing Adolphe Menjou and transmitted to the youthful Morris. Come to think of it, the youthful Morris is a bit like Adolphe himself, with those exquisite clothes, that hairline moustache, and those incipient side-whiskers, though Adolphe never wore the rimless glasses. All the same, Morrie's the ladies' man all right.

'How's Morrie?' Harry puts it to him in the third person aggressive.

Morrie, picking daintily at his nails with a penknife, lolls his head from side to side. This seems to betoken indifferent health, but Harry is seldom given to sympathy.

'Plate of beef – with a nice *lutkas*, yes? Or I've some very lovely tongues this morning. Listen, Morrie, I guarantee you these tongues are absolutely something special. You don't believe me, you should try them, eh? Wonderful.'

From the gravity and determination of Harry's manner you'd think he was trying to negotiate the Louisiana Purchase. But just to show his independence, Morrie settles for chopped liver and cheese-cake, with some lemon tea. And get that dainty arching of the finger when he lifts his glass, that perpetual flicking of those immaculate lapels. Yeah, Morrie certainly is the ladies' man.

Of course, they're not all like this. There's the doorman over there from the news cinema, just rolled in for a quick sandwich; and that negro standing by the urn, in the dungarees and the tartan windcheat, he's from the signwriter's studio next door. Usually there's a sprinkling of types from the stage door across the street and a few other regular characters, like Barney, the bookmakers' runner from off the corner. But mostly they're like Wolfie and Les and Morrie, bright, bandbox boys, well greased with external sophistication, yet never quite sure at any given moment whether to mimic Hollywood or St James's. It's a predicament, certainly. Maybe *that*'s what's been worrying Mr Goodman all this time.

'*The wife's borrowed mine – our pressure cooker's bust.*'

Lord Leighton

When Lord Leighton
Was tipped out of his phaeton
He landed in a position
Hardly suitable to an Academician.

A Matter of Taste

Bring me a lot
Of *saumon fumée en cocotte*;
Or failing the *saumon fumée*,
Cocotte will do me.

Cricket

I FIND it difficult to write dispassionately of cricket, not merely because I am an Englishman, but because Lord's is to me the most goddamned boring place in the whole of the British Isles. True, I have never been to a meeting of the Theosophical Society, or to the Lord Mayor's Banquet, but I am prepared to back my belief from what I have seen of Lord's during the moments when I have woken up to adjust my panama or to pass out in search of ale or other forms of relief.

Cricket, like many human failings, of which it is probably not the least harmful, is something as deep-rooted in the unconscious mind of the Englishman – at times a superb example of the comatose – as is his democratic sense, his indifference to politics, or his incomprehension of *chic*.

His feelings towards cricket are, as a rule, stronger than any of these, though not merely because they develop earlier than most of his other instincts. The reason is that the principles of the game are usually supposed to be those which afford mankind its best protection from the business end of life's harpoon. The cause and effect of *Magna Carta*, the elements of Liberalism, or the influence of Phidias on the Empire style, are not subjects of which a profound knowledge will sweep you through life with the ease of Mae West giving a *double entendre* to the words of Saint Francis. But the ability to send down a swift leg break or to hit that alarming phenomenon for six has its uses apart from cricket. A boot is better aimed at a cat if it is scientifically thrown, or a bailiff more easily parried with an umbrella if this be properly used for a forward drive or a cut to leg.

But there is not much hope of developing these capabilities unless the early feelings for cricket have been directed with care and encouragement. A great deal may happen, sometimes with deplorable results, if, during the kindergarten or dame school stage, these feelings are abandoned to the mercy of spinster tuition. The early enthusiasm may peter out or manifest itself in a preoccupation with arithmetic, or worse still,

'*Howzat!*'

music. But once the seeds of independent thought are sown, and have appeared in the amusing symbolism of the first long trousers, it is safe to assume that a proper esteem will be felt for the M.C.C.

Partly, perhaps, because my father was an oarsman and a scholar (and maybe too because my mother was a Boileau), there seems to have been some neglect of my cricketing education. At a time when the mystic relationship of the bat, the ball, and the bail should have been my preoccupation, I was

72

taken up with dubious and exotic thoughts of a completely different kind. The advertisements for Mazawattee Tea had pricked me into awareness that some higher form of beauty existed than I had been led to suppose from seeing Fragonard's *Pierrot* hanging on the nursery wall. The mysteries of the female form divine had presented themselves undeniably to me in picture postcards of Miss Marie Studholme and Miss Gertie Millar. Odd visits, ill-supervised by governesses yet more odd, to the waxworks at Madame Tussaud's had filled me with speculations about Wesley, General Gordon, Doctor Crippen, and Nell Gwynn. The women's suffrage movement was on foot, and while I played about on Hampstead Heath the mutinous squeals of Miss Sylvia Pankhurst echoed across the Whitestone Pond. No child who was not a cretin – and in spite of family arguments I was eventually allowed the benefit of the doubt – could have failed to wonder what was going on or to have been filled with faint, prophetic feelings of alarm.

But Miss Pankhurst was not the only attraction which the borders of the pond had to offer. In my childish and indiscriminate affections she took a bad second place to the tadpoles which I fished from the pale gravy where the dogs swam, the guttersnipes enviably paddled, and carts and horses waded in search of mild refreshment and adventure.

With Bleriot, Sexton Blake, and Charlie Chaplin as additional distractions, it may seem understandable that under the sporadic encouragement of my father, the scholarly oarsman (and my mother, the Boileau), my interest in cricket flagged from the very beginning. It was doubly unfortunate that when this subject was in the air all my childish hopes and energies were vested in an attempt to master the intricacies of roller skating. Those hours, which were few, when I was not floundering round the rink at Holland Park, saw me negligent and bored at cover point, a butter-fingers in the slips, or a timorous sullen rabbit skulking behind a pair of pads that would have served me as well for a shroud.

If at that time I found little enough to give me any enthusiasm for the game, I have since found a good deal that confirms my early opinion of it. But from those of my friends who are cricketers I have learnt beyond doubt that there is some secret, noble excitement in the game, though it is one from which I fear I must be for ever excluded through some lacking gland.

I can well imagine that cricket as it was played a hundred years ago must have been, like many other games, a much more friendly and jolly affair than it is today. To begin with, any form of vigorous exercise undertaken in a top hat seems to me to be fraught with amusing possibilities. Add to this the fun of using, as did one Surrey champion, 'a bat of preposterous width', and of tossing the ball down in the manner that is easiest, and the game becomes one that even the least athletic of us could play with enjoyment.

But somewhere about the year 1822 things began to go wrong, for that was the year in which John Willes, the Sutton Vallance player, was no-balled for 'throwing'. Willes, I am glad to say, showing a sense of humour in which the M.C.C. was – and still is – lacking, 'rode out of the ground, and out of the game for ever'.

'Scusi ...'

Punting

THERE are two things that should be remembered by everyone who wants to become puntworthy. One is NEVER to let go of the pole; the other is always to let go of the POLE. It is therefore best to travel, when travelling by punt, with two poles. One should be of standard length; the length of the other does not matter, though he or she should be of average weight and preferably able to speak English. An amusing alternative is that you should try to speak Polish.

If at any time you should need to part with one pole or the other, as an alternative to being what Mr Jeffrey Farnol would have called 'cleft in twain', the heavier pole is the one you should release. If the other pole, the one of standard length, is lost, then all is lost.

Whitaker's Almanack for 1931, which is the latest I have, tells me that the Doubles Punting Championship for the previous year was won by T. L. Hewett and H. R. Higginson. It tells me also that 'a fluid *drachm* is equal in weight to TWO avoirdupois *drams*'. But that, of course, was in 1931.

Fig. 1. *Type of pole in general use.*

Fig. 2. *Utterly useless type of Pole*

'I wish automation would make me redundant.'

'*Mark you, I have never given the slightest encouragement to either Bulganin or Khruschev.*'

Otter Hunting

OTTER HUNTING is rather fun, especially if you are not otter hunting but are there only to see what is going on. For, with the possible exceptions of croquet and the library of the British Museum, it brings out some of the oddest specimens of the sporting fraternity that you could or could not wish to see.

The otter, like Sir Alan Herbert, is a long brown thing which enjoys messing about on the river. It is a rather secluded animal, and a poignant character study of it has been made by Sir J. Arthur Thomson, who was at one time, I believe, Regius Professor of something or other at Aberdeen University, apparently without suffering any ill effects. From his sympathetic portrait of the otter it is clear that this sagacious creature is something of a matriarch, and is strongly opposed to any Montessori nonsense for juvenile otters. Though strict in its tutelage, it is liberal and far-sighted, and the curriculum which it sets up includes 'the fit and proper ways of diving and lying *perdu*, the methods of capturing different kinds of booty, and the recognized ways of eating trout, etc.'

In a higher, or possibly lower, social order the otter would clearly be 'something in the City'. All that has been said of it by Sir Arthur Thomson may be applied also to the gentleman to whom I entrust the mismanagement of my investments, and who, although he has yet to learn the recognized ways of eating trout, is in nearly all other respects hardly distinguishable from an otter.

The dogs, or more properly speaking, the hounds engaged for this sport – I am speaking now of otter hunting, not stock-broking – have rough hair and long silky ears. They are noisy and, worse still, indefatigable. After two or three hours of rapid loping through mud or wet grass, modified by occasional spurts or by leaping and wading, there comes a time when a halt would be welcome. As far as I am concerned this moment comes very early on, and as the hunt progresses the desire to be at home with a stiff whisky and soda and some Beethoven on the gramophone is almost insupportable. Of

'. . . how they run,
Through wood and mead, in shade and sun.'

course, there are many people who would consider that spurting and wading all through the night would be a lesser trial than having to listen to the *Eroica*. It is merely a matter of taste.

To some extent otter hunting is also a matter of smell. The hounds smell the otter, the otter smells the hounds – and do you know that peculiar, fusty smell of old cretonne, old copies of *The Times*, old plants, old biscuits, old marsala, and old retired colonels? That is the smell of otter hunting, and with it are compounded the scents of the river bank and of the colonel's lady. For here she comes, crashing through the king-cups in her tweeds and gaiters, booming at the hounds in a voice that is at once loud and husky, stabbing her neighbour in the ankle with a javelin, and barging aside everyone who stands in her path.

You may wonder, perhaps, what the otter has done to deserve all this. But what about the colonel?

'Is it part of it, or d'you think we should tell him?'

Hockey

ONE of the curious things about hockey is that no one has yet thought it worth while to interfere with the game and organize it on popular lines so that the whole thing may be turned into a limited company. That there must be some snag about it I do not doubt, but what this is I cannot think, for here there seems to be in every sense a virgin field.

Among many peculiar things about this game are the players. Though an average intelligence is no bar to your becoming a champion, you stand a better chance if you are distinguished also in economics, biology, or science. If you are not a girl, you probably will not bother about the game, unless you have ever been in the Japanese Army, of which hockey was once part of the athletic curriculum. But as this

'Pass, Gwyneth!'

83

seems to have included a number of things that are hardly likely to have been laid down in Mikado's Regulations, you are no doubt better off in the Civil Service, the *kosher* meat trade, or whatever your job happens to be. Incidentally, although the history of sport bristles with the names of Jewish champions, there has never been, so far as I know, a single instance of a Hebrew hockey star. The game seems to be limited not merely to the races of the northern hemisphere but almost exclusively to the Celts of this island, and more especially to those of Girton, Somerville, and Lady Margaret Hall.

Turning to pleasanter things, what of the history of hockey? In its present form the game dates from somewhere about 1885, when stiff collars, straw hats, leg-of-mutton sleeves, and leg-of-mutton mentalities decreed stern discomfort for such folly as playing an outdoor game. Before that, hockey was in a terrible mess, what with bits and pieces that had been tacked on to it during the preceding two thousand years by the Persians, who I believe had something to do with the start of it, the Portuguese, the Argentines, and the Greeks. Since then, of course, a certain amount of order has been introduced. The ball is now of standard diameter and weight, and the area of the field is specified by the rules, which also exclude the intrusion of bookies. The stick, and very often the player, has a flat face. She, unless a Japanese ex-Service woman, also has black woollen legs of impressive size and an expression which is forthright, serious, and though a little frightening in repose, yet more alarming when she laughs. She exists largely on cocoa, stringent moral principles, and firm friendships among her own sex and is not the sort of girl who would be seen at the Ritz Bar if the barman could help it.

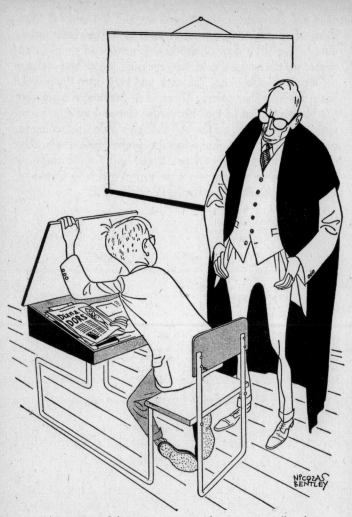

'Correct me if I'm wrong, Patterson, but I cannot recollect that
Diana Dors played any part in the Council of Trent.'

'*You goin' to Ascot this year?*'

Racing

ENGLISHMEN, in the fullness of their hearts, and saturated as they are with sentimentality about animals, have in a rather arbitrary way ennobled the horse above all other beasts. Why, with the sagacity of the chimpanzee, the fidelity of the elephant, and the humour, albeit of a somewhat cynical kind, evinced by the hyena – with all these to choose from, why the horse should have been regarded as the epitome of mammalian virtues is as mysterious as the Englishman's fondness for bowler hats, facetiousness, synthetic cheese, and the music of Eric Coates.

You might have thought the dog would rightly be the friend of man. But in point of fact it would be truer to say that it is primarily the pet of women. For Englishmen usually look upon dogs – and women – with an eye to their breeding capacities and sporting instincts.

Some men affect a feeling of closer kinship with dogs than with their own kind, in which no doubt they are right more often than they suspect. By lavishing affection on some sort of hound they are able to work off feelings which they are too gauche to express openly for the opposite sex. But women, especially those who dote upon objects as much resembling a bottle-brush or a *toupet* as a dog, are to a far greater extent responsible for the less dignified phases of dog nonsense.

The horse, though still primarily a beast of burden, has a certain nobility that is less easily discernible in, say, the goldfish. It is, for one thing, a more companionable animal, and though my knowledge of the cerebral processes of the goldfish is based largely on hearsay, I suspect that the horse is the more intelligent. It is also more easily able to arouse emotion in the human breast, a capacity seldom to be observed even among the most extrovert of goldfish. There can be few Eng-

'*Don't be silly, there's a credit squeeze on.*'

'Hey! She was only meant to kick off –'

lishmen whose blood, however sluggish, is not mildly stirred by the thought of setting off for the Derby or the Grand National. Even I, whose knowledge of horses is limited to the direction in which they are going, feel a perceptible increase in my own blood pressure. The movement is a faint one, but the prospect definitely induces an emotional if not corpuscular reaction; for I am not one to take a calm view of the chance to win a fiver, or the greater likelihood of losing one.

The British race, deemed often and rightly to be phlegmatic to a degree which makes the turtle seem intolerably vivacious, reacts towards certain phenomena with a startling and instinctive alacrity. The average Briton will jump as quickly at the chance of taking a bet as some American politicians at taking a bribe. With a knowledge of horseflesh derived wholly from the notes of so-called racing specialists, the so-called British working man will readily wager a large slice of his weekly earnings on the chances of a horse or jockey whom he has never set eyes on. The fact that bookmakers exist – a hideous conclusion in itself – on the perpetual optimism of such persons does not quench that same optimism in others or deter them from betting upon ventures as remote from the realities of their own existence as are the charms of a Javanese houri.

'THREE TO ONE BAR ONE!'

My Aunt Carrie, a better judge of horseflesh than most women – she judged them not upon their inherent nobility but upon their capacity for the work which God and the Jockey Club intended them to do – my Aunt Carrie held that you can usually tell a man from a horse because no horse would be such a fool as to back itself against odds fixed at anything from 10 to 100 to 1, when, logically speaking, odds which are incalculable cannot exist.

Lack of logic, however, is not the least of our racial peculiarities. We are also highly inconsistent. Our appetites are governed not by the laws of Nature but by those of Parliament; freedom of speech is a valued heritage, but freedom of what we may see and hear is limited by the arbitrament of a censor; and while we proclaim justice and humanity to be the basis of our laws, we permit some of these to offer to the rich offender freedom of choice in the matter of penalties, but to the poor no alternative but prison. Many Londoners who are as ignorant of horseflesh as I am make the annual and highly inconvenient pilgrimage to Epsom or Aintree without any compunction, though seldom in their lives do they go to the lesser bother of visiting Kempton Park or Sandown. The spectacle of the Grand National, of course, makes it an understandable attraction. But it is difficult to say why the Derby, whose surroundings are not a patch upon Goodwood's, and whose *éclat* is not comparable with that of Ascot, should have become a national rendezvous. It is one of those idiosyncrasies which make the Englishman, for all his matter-of-factness, as unpredictable as his own erratic weather.

We go to the Derby, said Ian Hay, in much the same spirit as we go 'to war or to bed, because at the moment there seems to be no possibility of anybody doing anything else'. For Ian Hay, perhaps, that may have been a good enough reason; for me it is at once an excuse for doing something entirely different. Perhaps it is that I am less gregarious than the average Englishman, that I am more reserved, misanthropic, and anti-social, but to me that great, voluble, friendly, sweating, addled mass known as the British public is less tolerable as a whole than when it is split up into individual souls, although in fairness it must be granted a kind of corporate benevolence, an instinctive love of justice, and a degree of common sense which are sometimes very reassuring.

To see the British public at the races is to see it at its best and its worst, chummy, argumentative, prudent, credulous, generous, and self-satisfied. Its enthusiasm for the sport is often negligible; but its enjoyment of betting is unparalleled in the dubious calendar of its amusements. Surely so great a faith in the benevolence of Fate must warrant some special kind of heaven for the British public hereafter? I am glad to think I shall be elsewhere.

On Mrs W—

Earth has not anything to show more fair
Than Mrs W—'s peroxide hair,
Nor anything intended to beguile,
And yet so charmless, as her constant smile.
Huge shining artificial gems encrust
Her huge though far from artificial bust;
And when she laughs her shrill and ringing tone
Is reminiscent of the telephone.
Her conversation, like Niagara Falls,
Engulfs the visitor in spray, and if it palls
This is because it would be hard to find
A tongue so loosely allied to a mind.

94

95

All the Fun of the Fair Sex

IN a mood of morbid contemplation which sometimes descends upon me like an umbrella closing unexpectedly over its owner's head, I have been considering the subject of women.

It is a large subject, and the capricious inclination of my thoughts rules out the discovery of any new and possibly disturbing truths. Not that I believe we are today any nearer to understanding what makes the mind of a girl tick than we were when Adam was in long fig-leaves. Do we, for instance, know any more now than he knew then about the instincts that make one girl a dutiful wife and mother and another a demirep? Or what it is, irrespective of circumstances, that will turn one young woman into a generous and easy-going bohemian, and another into a calculating gold-digger? We do not; though none of us – I speak as one who once was a gay and foolish youth, but who is gay and youthful no longer – who has ever escorted a platinum jane to the Four Hundred can have failed to learn something about gold-digging.

As far back as the Middle Ages this form of prospecting was second nature to women. When the philosopher's stone was the ultimate vision of the alchemist, they were employing their own already ancient processes for extracting gold not from stones but from men. And at this particular pastime women have excelled ever since. It would be ungenerous, though, to begrudge them success in this, for in almost every form of expression and exploitation of the mind the achievements of men are indisputably on a higher plane than those of women.

From this I except, of course, the miracle of birth, although repetition has now dulled our eyes to this achievement and the glamour that must once have attached to it has more or less worn off. Enterprising ladies, such as Mrs Dionne, have sought occasionally to re-impress us with the genius required of motherhood, but in few other fields, I think, can it be truthfully said that the achievements of women surpass those of men. Where, one may ask, are the feminine equals of Confucius, Homer, Michelangelo, Shakespeare, Napoleon, Rockefeller, or Miss Anna Pauker?

Admittedly women are still debarred from certain callings, either by the frailties of their own sex or the prejudices of mine. But in philosophy, government, commerce, science, and even in the arts, except those of interpretation, few have emerged who look like staying the hard course to posterity.

Whatever the reason for this, it is clear that something fundamental is at work, and I am sometimes tempted to wonder whether it may not be to do with the difference between

'Are you the new nurse? — 'cause if so I'm feeling far from well.'

97

'Who got the Nobel Prize?'

the male and female senses of humour; for in this, women, taking them by and large, and no offence meant, are as different as chalk from the cheese we knew in the days before it was processed.

Although on the whole women do not actively dislike joking – witness the phenomena often captured in marriage – they prefer wit, so long as it be of a not too savage kind, to ruder humours such as those of Chaucer and Rowlandson. With her subtler instincts a woman will often observe nuances of character and disposition that her husband may well fail to notice. Man, for instance, as seen through woman's eyes, usually stands at that point upon the arc of human behaviour where the sublime merges with the ridiculous. Not a very dignified position perhaps, but preferable to being an object of open amusement. A man's efforts to keep his balance will often provoke a sympathetic smile, sometimes even tinged with apprehension. It is when he loses it that the loud laughter comes. Man must therefore be ever on guard against those changes in the attitude and status of women by which the rather laughable forces of progress seek to undermine the edifice of his authority. In other words, he'd better watch out. If, in the process of equalizing their position, women get to have the same sort of sense of humour as men, we shall all be in a hot spot, we men. For this won't be just another change in women's taste, a caprice such as men have grown accustomed to meet with a weary smile and a blank cheque: it will be a change of mind on an alarming and unprecedented scale, a change in which all the hazards attendant on a woman changing her mind will be magnified beyond imagination.

Men may well become, in fact, not merely a part, but indeed all the fun of the fair sex.

'How's about a coupla ringsides for tonight, Jack?'

'I do so love it when autumn leaves begin to fall, don't you?'

Odd Man Out

THE other day, as I hurried down the steps of my bank, the cashier's laughter still ringing in my ears, an elderly man passed me on his way into the building.

He was obviously a man of substance. By his appearance you might have guessed him to be a retired member of some respectable business or profession; an importer of raw hides, perhaps, or an actuary, or a commissioner for oaths. Sedate, unobtrusive, even commonplace to look at, you would hardly have noticed him but for two small peculiarities. Not content with wearing one pair of glasses on top of another, he had a third pair poking out of his breast pocket, and round his neck a pair of pince-nez was hanging on a cord.

Now I am not one to remark uncharitably, I hope, on the foibles of other people, being all too conscious of my own. The Turkish slippers which I sometimes forget to take off until, too late, I find myself wearing them in the bus; the abstracted combing of my hair at mealtimes or in church: the umbrella carried while bathing. Such trifles, only significant to me of absent-mindedness, may strike others as eccentric. How, then, could I regard the idiosyncrasies of my fellow men with anything but a sympathetic smirk?

Yet I submit that to carry, if not to wear, four pairs of glasses all at once, is the action of an eccentric. If, in this case, corroboration were needed, a glance at the old man's hat would have given it away. Not that it was in any way a remarkable hat. Size six-and-seven-eighths I should have guessed it to be; in bat's-wing brown with a matching binding and a band to tone. In the band was a ticket showing the price – thirty-nine and six. Call it what you will in the name of charity, he who wears four pairs of spectacles and carries a price tag in his hat for all the world to see is undoubtedly a rummy.

'Kiss me, Hardy.'

As one gets older it is an uncomfortable thought to realize how faint, how intangible is the borderline between what seems normal and what is considered eccentric. The young are seldom eccentric, unless intentionally so; and conscious eccentricity is merely affectation. How and when does one become an eccentric? Surely there must have been a time when the old gentleman I had passed going into the bank would have thought it odd to carry four pairs of glasses, even on the grounds of safety first? When did it cease to be a matter of importance that he should conceal the price of his hats from an inquisitive public?

Such indifference, or such negligence if you prefer it, suggests more than a change of habit and more than mere forgetfulness. It shows a change in the attitude of mind which must cause one to hesitate before stopping in the street or in the middle of a conversation in order to take one's pulse, which was a regular thing with Mr Herbert Spencer.

It was also his practice, when travelling by train, to lie suspended in a hammock which he had slung across the carriage. Assuming the sage to have enjoyed a brief period of rollicking youth, there would have been a time, perhaps, when public pulse-taking or the conveyance of philosophers by first-class hammock must have seemed to him something out of the ordinary. What, then, caused such actions to assume, for him, the appearance of normality? Or though they may have seemed queer, not to matter nor seem incompatible with his dignity?

Advancing years and the decay of one's faculties may partly explain the development of eccentricity. One compensation for growing old is that externals tend to matter less as time goes on. But there have been, and still are, renowned eccentrics whose idiosyncrasies have bloomed and flourished even before middle age. Such a one was Jack Mytton, the Shropshire madcap, dead as a door-nail at thirty-eight. Beckford, like Chesterton, and Thoreau too, was unconsciously eccentric from early manhood. Hester Stanhope's peculiarities were apparent before she was thirty, and those of the learned Doctor Porson even earlier.

In *The English Eccentrics* Dame Edith Sitwell has hit, I think, on part of the truth. 'Eccentricity exists particularly in the English,' she says, 'and partly, I think, because of that peculiar and satisfactory knowledge of infallibility that is the hallmark and birthright of the British nation.'

So being an eccentric has less to do perhaps with age or infirmity of mind than with independence of spirit. It is difficult to imagine, for instance, that even the mildest sorts of eccentricity would have been tolerated in Nazi Germany. To express a liking for Picasso, which to most Englishmen seems a more than fantastic quirk, could hardly have been less dangerous under Hitler than to express disillusionment with the Nazi régime.

The true eccentric is not to be confused, though the mistake is often made, with the professional *poseur*. Wilde, like Whistler, his most serious competitor for notoriety, was not an eccentric in Dame Edith's sense of the word. His conduct may have been fanciful, but it was not the behaviour of a genuine eccentric. It expressed no more than was visible on the surface. While there was a responsive or incredulous eye to watch, his conduct was calculated with regard to the impression he hoped it would make. For Wilde, as for Brummell, there were no ends in life; there were only means. A too scrupulous regard for manners, or an impudent repudiation of

them, studied in either case for its effect, was part of the gesture that was Brummell's existence. For what existence had he
beyond the legend of his manners?

Eccentricity is not a gesture, unless it be continued after you
have become aware of it. As soon as I become aware that I am
sprinkling salt on my pudding, or that my trousers are on back
to front, I take steps to rectify the position. But who knows,
the day may come when I shall walk abroad, conscious but
careless of the fact that my panama is crushed about my ears
by the weight of winter snows, that the cords of my dressing
gown are awash in the gutter, and that the bag of bullseyes
under my arm is spilling its contents for my cockatoo to pick
up as it follows me.

I say, no doubt I shall be aware of these things. All the same,
if we should happen to meet, I should be glad if you would at
least mention the cockatoo.

Theme and Variations

'I never thought I'd get a holiday at all this year.'

Words for Ballet

'In a glitter, as if vociferous, of music, amid the very knees
of a climax, the male dancer revolves with *tours en l'air* . . .'
ADRIAN STOKES in *Tonight the Ballet*

ALTHOUGH ballet, as we know it, has been in existence for
almost fifty years, the streptococcus of balletptomania seems
to be of comparatively recent germination. Even more recent
is the discovery – it was made, I suppose one might say, during
the thirties – of how serious the effects of balletptomania may
become. Though there are few recorded instances of it having
proved fatal, I did once see a gentleman borne out from a performance of *Job* on a stretcher; in the opinion of the barmaid,
however, it was not *Job* but Johnny Walker that had proved
his undoing.

Among balletptomanic symptoms during the thirties was a
feverish output of writing, much of it as obscure as Einstein's

theory but lacking its validity. It is difficult to imagine, for instance, that the passage I have quoted with an ill-concealed grin at the beginning of this piece could have been written nowadays, or that even the most intense balletptomaine could take it seriously. Perhaps no one took it very seriously at the time. To me, at any rate, it still seems a pretty fair example of this kind of writing at its worst, or if you prefer it, at its best. That is to say, it is transcendental without being turgid, because it is also profoundly comic. Writing of this sort is usually characterized by a refreshing freedom from sense as well as from syntax. Mr Stokes's book is no exception to this class of literature. There is something about its imagery which reminds one of *Kubla Khan*'s obscurity or of the inconsequence of *Alice in Wonderland*. I am very fond of Mr Stokes's picturesque phrase, 'amid the knees of a climax'. This pleasing variation on the cliché about 'the horns of a dilemma' is clearly the writing of a balletptomaine of a high order.

The psychology of balletptomania is strange and interesting. Its causes and effects, its problems and peculiarities, are of a nature special to the disease, which is to be compared with no other form of dementia known to medical or Christian science. Even now, comparatively little is known about it, except that it is contagious and sometimes chronic, although as a rule its results are fairly harmless. Like hay fever, it is seasonal, appearing at the first sign of the ballet's approach; and like calf love there seems to be no cure for it but to let it work its way out of the system. In its advanced stages it takes the form of an inexplicable malaise which, at the mere mention of the ballet, seems either to paralyse or convulse what may be an otherwise well-balanced intellect. The name of Petipa, for instance, of Pavlova, Nijinsky, or Diaghilev, will often induce a reaction of incoherence and affectation beside which Joyce's *Anna Livia Plurabelle* takes on a semblance of lucidity.

Few balletptomaines seem to have escaped some degree of infection. Professor Arnold Haskell, whose illimitable plumb-

*'She says they've cried off the Chelsea Arts, will we meet them
at the Dorchester instead.'*

line must have sounded the depths of ballet lore almost to the
bottom, is not always free from traces of the germ. And even
Mr Cyril Beaumont's ardour has occasionally betrayed him
into a departure from that detachment which distinguishes so
large a part of his criticism from the hot air that escaped from
many an early enthusiast. Apart from Professor Haskell's
probings, however, there have been few contributions of
worth in the field of balletptomanic psychology, but this is
not for want of trying. In the early days of ballet criticism a
shower of wind and pebbles shot forth from almost every
balletptomaine capable of utterance. Isadora Duncan was a
dancer of unique reputation, and her words, however obscure,
cannot be dismissed without some consideration.

To my lasting regret, I never had an opportunity of seeing

her dance, but in the judgement of some who did, and on whose opinions I feel I can rely, her unique reputation was fully justified. I see no justification, however, for the nebulous theoretical jargon which she used to express her own ideas and feelings about dancing. In an essay on the subject, in which she describes a dance called *The Light Falling upon White Flowers*, she speaks of it as 'a translation of the light and the whiteness – so pure, so strong, that people would say, "It is a soul we see moving, a soul that has reached the light and found the whiteness." ' If that is, in fact, what Miss Duncan would have expected people to say, I am afraid she placed too high a trust in human nature. That some meaning was intended, I do not doubt; but what her meaning was escapes me, as it escaped her first audience. After her debut in Chicago, 'the general conclusion arrived at, after hours of acrimonious argument, was that the young woman had an idea, but that clairvoyancy was required to understand it'. It is quite clear that, as regards her dancing, this opinion was reversed by her later success. What

'Here's Daddy, darling, run and get the screwdriver.'

puzzles me is how an artist of such unusual gifts could so far suspend her self-critical faculties as to talk such rot.

But let us turn again to Mr Adrian Stokes, who presents the student of balletptomania with an engrossing case. It is symptomatic of this complaint that as the ballet season approaches the victim drifts into a sort of cataleptic ecstasy. I presume that it was under the influence of some such emotion that Mr Stokes produced the incoherent but, to the student, absorbing abstraction I have already quoted, and while under a similar attack no doubt that the following thesis was evolved: 'If you prod a piece of liver preparatory to cooking,' says Mr Stokes, 'it seems to bite back on the fork with a curious stringy bite. I can think of no sensation more different than the one Tchaikovsky's ballet music inspires.' This is almost the only point upon which I find myself wholly in agreement with the author. Would Mr Stokes, I wonder, think it a

'I told you about that last year!'

fair appraisal of Corot were I to say: 'When I hit grandpapa
with a tomato it exploded, and so did grandpapa. But this did
not in the least remind me of Corot's paintings'? The analogy
is perhaps a little far-fetched; but it is essentially the same as
the example which it parodies, in that it does not really help
one to understand the paintings of Corot any better than Mr
Stokes's confused symbolism helps to explain the *Fifth Sym-
phony*.

The complications of the Stokes theory for expounding
Tchaikovsky's intentions are presently carried a step further
into oblivion by the suggestion that the music is 'white, firm,
yet crisp'. Somewhere amid the inner recesses of Mr Stokes's
consciousness, there seems to be a still, small voice, like that of
Bunthorne's, which assures him that 'the meaning doesn't
matter, if it's only idle chatter of a transcendental kind'.
Pressing on, he presently gets to grips again with the piece of
crisp, white liver. But here there is a disappointment in store;
Mr Stokes is foiled. For it seems that this is not the kind of

liver you can 'prod with the mind'. As a matter of fact, so long as the mind continues to function, there seems to be no reason against using the conventional fork. But to appreciate the other treasures which Mr Stokes has found cunningly hidden in Tchaikovsky's music, every stop in the imagination must be pulled out. I'll bet you didn't know, for instance, that it had 'a white or silvery languor, a vast silvery thunder, stage-thunder, perhaps, though not the stage-thunder of tea trays, but of the Tsar's packed sideboards of silver'. And I'll bet Tchaikovsky didn't know it either.

Closing our ears to the din of the Tsar's thundering sideboards, and opening our minds in preparation for fresh surprises, we find that what Mr Stokes calls 'the outwardness of the ballet', combined with its 'geometry' and 'the harmonious gradualness of its forms, is an emblem of the European spirit'. Failing to grasp what is meant by the 'outwardness' or the 'geometry' of ballet, I also failed, of course, to understand their relation to the European spirit. It is only fair

'Well, saves having my tooth out.'

to Mr Stokes, and to the European spirit, to remind oneself that *Tonight the Ballet*, whence I crib these *bonnes bouches*, appeared at a time when all was comparatively harmonious in Europe. It was, so to speak, an era of friendship all round. Hitler was courting Mussolini, Mussolini was blowing kisses to Franco, Franco was ogling Laval, and what Laval was up to with Sammy Hoare, as he then was, was nobody's business, least of all the Abyssinians'.

It may well be, as Mr Stokes seems to imply, that the 'outwardness' and 'geometry' of the ballet, the 'harmonious gradualness of its forms', were indeed emblematic of all these goings on. I wonder, though, whether these emblems still represent the European spirit; or whether, like so many other things that might have been said – with an even stricter regard for truth – to represent the long and liberal view of human purpose, Mr Stokes's emblems have not become meaningless shibboleths in the light of history; that is, of course, if they were not meaningless shibboleths already. Where, for instance, shall we look for this 'harmonious gradualness' today? Where for the 'outwardness'? – which, if it meant *Lebensraum* before (and if it didn't, your guess is as good as mine), must now mean 'expansion'. Where shall we look for its 'geometry'?

Yes, there is something about the ballet which seems to induce a kind of hypnosis in some of its critics, and while under this spell there is no knowing what a critic may do or say. Who could have imagined, for instance, that Mr Rayner Heppenstall, in his *Apology for Dancing*, would let fly with such a shaft as this? – 'Ballet is a continuing struggle – of mind against matter, you might say, but rather of general against particular. It derives from, and subsists in, tensions. With the dancer, it is a struggle between a wastefully complex muscular

'*Dug up! You're always wanting to be dug up. Why can't you let the the child enjoy himself?*'

system, designed for a limited range of animal acts and offices, and the economy, the simplicity, in line and mass, of the postures and movements,' etc., etc.

Wiping the tears from our eyes, we read on to make the startling discovery that 'with the spectator, it is a struggle between the rigid habit of his eye and the need to contemplate his perceptions musically, a struggle resolved through kinaesthetic response, through muscular sympathy, nervous empathy, inscape. Ballet must be felt by the spectator in that way. Ballet, viewed as a structure, a system of tensions, is human beings behaving in the Manner of Music.'

I am all for everyone behaving in the Manner of Music, particularly such music as that of *Knocked 'em in the Old Kent Road* or *Auprès de ma blonde*. But I am against anyone behaving in a manner that reduces criticism to a point where it becomes so difficult to follow that little profit is to be had from reading it. There is plenty of room for theoretical argument about ballet without coming to loggerheads over 'geometry' or 'nervous empathy'. As a matter of fact, I suffer a good deal from nervous empathy myself; so, unlike some of the critics I have quoted, I know what I'm talking about.

You need to be careful about nervous empathy; don't let your feet get wet; keep out of draughts; and, above all, no celery. A bad attack may leave you depressed and irritable for months. I remember there was an outbreak some years ago among the company in which Fallova was then appearing at Covent Garden. She had found me a place back-stage one evening, from which I was to watch *Les Femmes de Bonne Humeur*. When we arrived upon the scene another ballet was in progress. Fallova led me over to where *Les Femmes* were sitting, and I must say, a more disagreeable-looking set of girls I have never met. I sat down next to one of them and by way of breaking the ice in which her *bonne humeur* seemed imprisoned I said, 'You don't feel nervous?'

'*We must apologize to viewers for a technical hitch . . .*'

'*'Ullo, I see the Four Power talks 'ave started.*'

'Why should I?' she said. 'You look harmless enough.'

To this I could think of no appropriate riposte, and even had there been one, the breath for its delivery was knocked clean out of me by Woizikovsky, who at that moment made a prodigious leap into the wings and landed slap on top of me. Woizikovsky, the chair, and I went down like a pack of cards, dashing several other dancers to the ground as we fell. By the time I had been helped to my feet, dusted, and straightened out, the ballet had ended, and *Les Femmes de Bonne Humeur* was about to begin.

Furious activity reigned all round, and none more furious than between *Les Femmes* themselves, whose mute hostility towards each other now broke out in fisticuffs and oaths. Without warning, I found that I was suddenly whirling round in the middle of a crowd of enraged ballerinas, striking out indiscriminately at me and at each other.

The whole thing had started literally in a flash, and in a flash it ended. With my eyes tight shut and my head down, I was milling out in all directions, when I suddenly realized that the pummelling and scuffling which had been going on around me had stopped. I opened my eyes cautiously and found I was alone in the middle of the stage, striking out into space, accompanied by the orchestra who were playing the opening bars of the music. The sight of the audience was almost as much of a shock to me as my appearance must have been to them. There seemed to be only one thing for it; and

'*Dr Hoffmeyer is absolutely brilliant.*'

that was to pretend, which I did, that it was all part of the ballet. I waltzed round several times, feinting and posturing rather feebly, and feeling a complete b.f. By introducing a few impromptu *jetés* and *glissades* I managed to bring myself near the side of the stage, and then decided to jump for it. As I did so, the cue came for Youpushoff's entrance, and he hurtled from the wings with a magnificent leap of several yards. We met in mid-air, chest to chest, with a crash that would have knocked the stuffing out of a turkey. An exquisite firmament of stars appeared in front of me as I described a lightning parabola and came to rest with my head cushioned in Youpushoff's posterior.

I have never danced at Covent Garden since that night.

André Gide

Liberty and Licence

Blessed are the rich
Who can afford the clubs
Where they go on drinking
When the poor have left the pubs.

André Maurois

André Maurois seems to me
All that a Frenchman ought to be,
Witty, cultured, and by Jingo!
Has the sense to speak our lingo.

Reflections on the Blue Boy

WHILE I was at the Turkish baths the other day, the slab on the slab next to mine began to discuss Art. The masseur who was attending me at once pricked up my ears, and before long the baths were ringing with the immortal monickers of Giotto, Tintoretto, Leonardo, Canaletto, old Uncle El Greco, and all. Presently, the mention of Gainsborough's name reminded me of his Blue Boy, whose appearance we remember so well, but of whose life we know so little.

Musing on my slab, thick-coming fancies crowded in upon my mind. Who was he, this dark and introspective youth? And what became of him? Perhaps, as the years advanced, and in appreciation of the greatness Gainsborough thrust upon him, he may have conceived the delicate compliment of dyeing his whiskers with cobalt: and if, as might well have been the case, he was a sensuous lad, living in an age of cruelty and careless morals, the case may seem plain for his identification as the original Blue Beard.

This, however, I believe to be a fallacy, for I have another theory, and though I would not claim it to be irrefutable, taken in connexion with the facts, such as they are, I warm to the idea of its probability.

We of the *cognoscenti* know this much of Gainsborough's model: that his name, like that of his father, was Jonathan Buttall; that he lived in Soho, and was in later life – perhaps even as a child, though this seems less likely – an ironmonger; and that he was said to have died immensely rich.

Not much to go on, perhaps; yet nothing, on the other hand, to refute my assumption of the youth's identity: there can be little doubt, in my opinion, that Jonathan Buttall, Jnr, and little Boy Blue were *one and the same*. It is true that no horn is visible in his picture, nor any cows or sheep; nor is he depicted under a haycock fast asleep. But it is precisely the *absence* of these

125

features in Gainsborough's masterpiece that, to my mind, confirms beyond doubt the identity of his sitter.

Let us examine these points in turn. Why is there no horn? May it not have been that momentarily the snob in Gainsborough peeped out? That in his impatience to begin on the Duchess of Devonshire, the penny trumpet of a shepherd lad was sacrificed to the plumes of the *haute monde*? 'But, good Gad, Tom!' I hear Reynolds crying, 'where is the boy's horn?'

And Gainsborough with a shadow of impatience answers, 'What d'you mean, "where's the horn"? It's under his cape; you can't see it, that's all.'

'Can't see his crook, either,' ventures Romney joining in shyly, with a wink at Hoppner.

And Gainsborough, conscious perhaps of that peeping snob, and a little ashamed of it, takes refuge in indignation.

'Well, what more d'you expect? Want all the sheep in, too, I suppose? And the haycock! You think I'm going to sweat my guts out on a lousy little brat of a –'

'Tush, Tom! –' says Reynolds, and goes down like a log under Gainsborough's impatient fist.

Personally I reject this line of argument. Gainsborough was little, if anything, of a snob, and though neurotic, he was a man of equable temper. No, I fancy we must look elsewhere to explain the missing features of this portrait. Let us look instead at the words, *Come, blow up your horn!* We are struck immediately by something strange, something at first glance unfathomable in the phrase. Why 'blow *up* your horn'? Why not just 'blow' it? Why not 'sound' it, or 'toot' it? Even 'wind your horn' would be permissible, if we allow a certain amount of poetic licence in the matter of how a horn is played. The answer is, I believe, that this particular horn was not a horn of brass, but was a powder-horn.

At once the true meaning of that hitherto obscure remark is illuminated. 'Blow *up* your horn!' The cows are already in the meadow, remember, breaking the fences, trampling down the new-dug ditches, tearing with greedy muzzles at the hedgerows and at the half-finished stacks; and in the cornfield the sheep are vandals, trampling the precious ears, the virgin stalks, wrecking the harvest that was to have been. Ruination is staring the farmer in the face. But where *is* the farmer? The farmer is asleep in bed, and the farmhouse lies a good league hence (or am I thinking of King Wenceslas?). Anyway, the farmer is too far off and too far gone to be roused by a little tin trumpet. A thunderclap is needed and Little Boy Blue must blow up his horn!

The courageous boy, ignoring the dangers of the cavorting herd, kneels down beside a stook and lays the trail. Daisy, a brindled Hereford of doubtful pedigree, comes along behind him and licks it up as he moves forward, so back he has to go to lay it all over again. He leaves in the horn itself a powerful charge, then dashes back to shoo Daisy off the trail once more. He lights his tinder-box and shields the guttering flame with a hand which quivers like his own Adam's apple. The flame is

'Why stand so close?'

set to the powder, and in a moment the breeze has carried the fire forward. There is a *roar* ... cows and sheep fall piecemeal from the sky; the stunned youth, clambering to his feet, is clouted down again with a fine shoulder of mutton and gets a beef brisket in the bread-basket.

The farmer, a man of pious instincts and guilty conscience, wakes up in a panic, thinking his last hour is at hand. He falls out of bed on to the floor and tries to scrabble underneath the wardrobe. The wardrobe falls over on to the bed and buries the farmer's wife in the bolster, revealing unto him in his hour of need that out of evil cometh good.

There can be little doubt, I think, that the Blue Boy's absence of cows and sheep may be accounted for by some such catastrophe as this. It would explain, too, the disappearance of his crook, his faithful sheep-dog (blown to smithereens, of course), and the other appurtenances of shepherdhood. It would explain the murky and disordered landscape, as well as the youth's pale face and look of slight anxiety; though here, perhaps, we tread on more supposititious ground.

Adolescence is a troubled time, and Buttall, Jnr, was in the pink of it (or, should I say, the blue?) when Gainsborough painted him. Might not the Blue Boy's slightly apprehensive yet inquiring gaze signify the turbulence of a youthful conscience struggling with the base realities of life? The child is father to the man, and the rich ironmonger in embryo was perhaps filled already with an ironmonger's hopes, an ironmonger's fears, and an ironmonger's lusts. But ironmongers do not lust merely for bolts and bars, or for curtain rings and galvanized iron watering cans; not unless their case history is under analysis by Kraft-Ebbing. They are human with the weaknesses of humans, and there is no reason to suppose Buttall, Jnr, was an exception. Rather the reverse, in fact. Look at his features: weakness portrays itself in every line of them; vacillation stares out from the canvas; even his attitude shows indecision, a foot half pointed, as if he were retrieving with uncertainty the false start of a cotillon. Clearly he is a lad as

'Now, is that the same trick that your grandfather saw?'

weak as water, a tool, a very cat's-paw. No wonder he was left standing while the rest romped off to the *fête champêtre*, their gay, their cruel laughter ringing in his ears. Poor Jonathan Buttall, Jnr!

Yet even in the hour of his humiliation, such is the equity of providence, there comes a chance to redeem the fatal weaknesses of his character. The shouts and laughter die upon the wind and for a while all is silent. Presently the boy's ears detect another sound, a strange rumbling, as of a dyspeptic giant. The distant thud of approaching cattle, the patter of maddened hooves gathers and grows; all in a moment the boy is overwhelmed.

He rises, with his plumed hat jammed over his ears, from the ditch where he has been flung, and is straightway tossed across the hedge and then tossed back again. He lights on a ram and is borne off, jolting very fast, and is then bucked into the air. Now the strong voice of courage whispers to him, and on the instant, he prepares the trail and then explodes his horn.

But what is this dark shape crouched in the ditch? A shape that watches with darting eyes and which sets down in a little notebook every detail of the frantic scene? Is it the village Constable? No; it is the village Gainsborough, out for a walk before breakfast; a rare occurrence for Gainsborough, who liked to lie a-bed. What fortuitous summons brought him forth so early on this particular morning we shall never know. Man in the full flower of his imagination, man with his artifice, with all his fine-drawn perceptions of nature, may yet find inspiration for his sublimest works in the casual gestures of chance.

I wonder if it would interest you to know what the Laughing Cavalier was laughing at? It's a fascinating story ...

'*Are you going to Glyndebourne this year?*'

'I realize that, madam, but the cost of dying has gone up too.'

'You haven't a Santa Claus by Picasso?'

Origins of Santa

To all of us comes sooner or later the realization – and it is often a rather painful one – that something in which we have believed implicitly since the dawn of understanding is after all nothing but a myth. The paths of history are strewn with the remains of idols that were found to have had feet of clay or, as in the case of the late Lord Baldwin, for instance, of French chalk, a more friable substance and one which lends itself to the preparation of whitewash.

I don't know what it was that first aroused my suspicions about Santa Claus, but I remember finding it difficult to reconcile the gas-fire that blocked the nursery hearth with the legend of his descent from the chimney. Or perhaps it was that on one of his visits he had a bad attack of hiccups. On another occasion, I remember, he stubbed his toe against the bed and a volley of oaths resounded in the darkness. Although

I can scarcely have been a day more than seventeen at the time, from that moment I began seriously to question the reality of his existence. Later researches proved – to my satisfaction, anyway – that the whole thing is a two-fold myth. For one thing there never was such a character; and for another, any resemblance he may be thought to have had to Lord Woolton with a false beard clipped round his ears is entirely co-incidental.

The known facts about Santa Claus – and no doubt about Lord Woolton – are simple and few. To start with, he was a Greek, which, of course, was not his fault. He was also a bishop – of Myra in Lycia, and unlike some bishops who could do with it, he was put to the torture and imprisoned. At one time he apparently went about claiming the acquaintance of Athanasius, whom he said he had met at the Council of Nicaea. However, Athanasius replied that he'd never set eyes on him, which made him look rather a fool. All this happened while Greece was groaning under the despotic sway of Diocletian, mention of whom reminds me of an interesting and I believe hitherto unrevealed fragment of biographical information:

> *The Emperor Diocletian*
> *Stuffed himself to repletion,*
> *Yet never felt, as one so often feels,*
> *Sensations of discomfort after meals.*

Some time after Santa Claus's death, or to be more accurate, during the comparatively temperate reign of Justinian, he was awarded a halo. In 1087 the inhabitants of Bari, having nothing better to do, rose as one man and seized the episcopal corpse, which they brought home with them, and afterwards erected a basilica there in Santa's honour. Incidentally, for those of a statistical turn of mind there is food for thought in the fact that in England alone there are some four hundred places of worship dedicated to his memory; while at Istanbul there stands a church associated jointly with him and another

134

'Have you decided where you're going for your holidays?'

saintly codger rejoicing in the unlikely name of Priscus. Little
is known, it seems, about this character except that:

> *The blood of St Priscus*
> *Was extraordinarily viscous.*
> *When his nose bled it took the drip*
> *About an hour to reach his lower lip.*

In this respect he seems to have been rather the opposite of
Santa whose blood was up at the drop of a mitre where there

was the slightest suspicion of injustice or of anyone jumping the queue, as for instance, when deciding who should be thrown to the lions first.

Though I should like to feel that there is something of this rudely handled patriarch's nobility in my own nature, something of the insouciance with which his kind habitually wear their tops hats inverted, I do not really feel there would have been much in common between Santa and me. There is no beam of rosy and perpetual benevolence in the cheesed-off countenance that stares at me from the shaving mirror in the mornings. I do not, as a matter of course, dress in gum-boots and red flannel trimmed with cotton wool; and such reindeer as I have come across have left me with a marked feeling of dislike for their species. However, there is one particular in which Santa Claus and I share a resemblance; we have the same Christian name. His surname is unknown, but I feel it would be too much of a coincidence to suppose that it might have been Bentley.

Among the posthumous distinctions conferred upon him was that of being appointed the patron saint of children. He also became the patron saint of scholars and sailors and, rather surprisingly, of merchants, which is presumably why at Christmas time you may see him slouching round Harrods, Selfridges, Gamages, etc. No doubt this accounts also for his insignia – three golden orbs, or brass balls – as seen in the picture of him by Raphael, in which he is shown scanning the fixture list with a rather dubious expression before kicking off with one of the gilded orbs.

His patronage of children leads to his often being depicted with three of them stuffed into a barrel at his side. This seems an excellent way of dealing with the problems of paternity, even though the children with whom he appears are usually shown standing the right way up.

When the Dutch, in their ignorance, began migrating to America, they took with them as a symbol of Yuletide beneficence the image of San Nicolaas. It was but the work of a moment for the natives to transform these euphonious syllables into Sanner Klars, which, with appropriate variations (e.g. Polynesian, *Saa'n Ti Kai-Laos*; Eskimo, *Santik Los*) is the name by which he is still known today.

And now it only remains for me to wish you and Lord Woolton a Happy Christmas.

Casual Acquaintance

'ISN'T Bea Lillie *ab*solutely wonderful?' I agreed that she was, not that any answer was needed. He prattled on, standing wedged between the buffet and the door, his cigarette holder in one hand and his sherry glass in the other. He was tall and rather good-looking. His round amber-coloured eyes never stayed still for a moment as long as he was talking. When I spoke they bored into me as though my every word was purest gold; nothing goes down so well as being a really good listener.

'Where are you going for Christmas?' he asked. I said I wasn't going anywhere, which of course was quite the wrong answer. He was tactful. 'Aoh, but I do envy you. Going away at Christmas time *is* such a bore.' He was going down to his mother in Wiltshire. She had a house that was quite close to Cecil's. In fact he'd probably run over some time and see him, unless Cecil ran over to him. A rather attractive picture floated into my mind of their running gracefully towards each other. He went on about the house. It was '*the* most lovely old stone house with a quite perfect garden – aoh, thank you *so* much!' Teeth and eyes flashed as the hired waiter, a nice-looking chap, approached once more with the drinks. I took another martini. I could see I had done the wrong thing. With the choice of martini, sherry, or champagne I should have known better.

However, back to Mummy's exquisite tomb on the Wiltshire downs. It seemed she had four (indoor) servants, though why I should be interested in her domestic arrangements wasn't clear. Two of them had known him since he was a small boy, if that's what he once was. He was the sort whom servants dote on, of course; the sort who's awfully good with them. You could tell that from the way he had smiled at the hired waiter, so frank and so friendly.

Ars vita, longa brevis

Talk turned to the Royals. 'Don't you *adore* Margaret?' I do
as a matter of fact, but the way it was said made me feel that
I didn't want to admit it. He'd been to the do at Blenheim, of
course, and had flown over to Paris for Balmain's show as well.
I decided to jump in at this point and tell him about the wholesale dress parade in Eastcastle Street that I'd covered for the
agency last week. His indifference was beautifully veneered.
He was still jammed in between the buffet and the door, wilt-
ing slightly, like an overgrown indiarubber plant, but as I

couldn't move either, he couldn't get out. So we made the best of a bad job and skipped to literature, or to be more precise, to Willie Maugham and she whom he preferred to call

la belle Compton-Burnett. And so to music, meaning, inevitably, *Troilus and Cressida*, the Harewoods, and good old Eddie Sackville-West. I asked if he'd heard that someone was writing an account of Sir Malcolm's trip to Tokyo, and was going to call it 'Flash in Japan'. That nearly threw him, but not quite.

'*Aoh*, but how wonderful!' he said, but the smile was rather glazed. I gathered he and Sir Malcolm had never met.

Presently it was time to go. I flattened myself against the

unyielding rump of a woman of title so as to make enough room for him to ooze forth. Gradually he insinuated himself towards our hostess. I followed. We made our adieux, mine in terms that sounded brief and austere in comparison with his, and then fought our way into the street.

'Have you got a car?' I asked. 'Alas, no. I don't drive.' I might have known it. 'Can I give you a lift then? I'm going towards Hammersmith.' I was really going to Chiswick Mall, but I was feeling sadistic by this time. I wanted to see him wince and I wasn't disappointed. 'If you *could* drop me – *any*-where near West Halkin Street.' 'Of course,' I said. 'Aoah, you *are* kind.'

It seemed he was staying in a friend's flat while the friend was in Rome. Apparently it was *too* lovely. I wondered what it was too lovely for. Clearly not for him. There was *the* most *fas*cinating piece of *trompe l'œil*, and a wonderful, but *wonder*-ful, Aubusson that had belonged to Bernhardt, imagine! And *aoh*, the *pictures*! As a matter of fact, he'd been frightfully wicked that afternoon: he'd bought – he hadn't *meant* to, it was just that he was *in* Sotheby's and simply couldn't resist it – a *most* lovely gouache by Guardi. (The accent, need I say, was authentically Venetian.) He would *so* love me to see it. Per-haps I could come in some evening for a drink. He was only dashing back for a moment now to change – did I know Princesse Chavchavardzé? – he was dining with her at the Connaught. I wondered whether to tell him where I was dining and with whom: at the Nosh Bar in Windmill Street with a fellow who makes machine tools and lives in Rugby. But I didn't. I felt he'd had about as much as he could stand for one evening.